Paradise Circus: A Birmingham Miscellany

www.paradisecircus.com

First published by Paradise Circus in 2014.
Copyright © Paradise Circus 2014.

Set in a grown-up, Brummie font: Baskerville.

The authors assert the moral right to be identified as the authors of this work, whatever that means.

A catalogue record for this book is available from the British Library. A Kay's catalogue record player is available from your Mom's book.

ISBN 978-1-78280-399-7

101 Things Birmingham Gave The World

This book is dedicated to the memory of the Birmingham Central Library.

So. Farewell
Then
Central Library
John Madin's ziggurat

You were a huge
Building
With books in.

But that was not
Your only purpose.

You stood for
Ambition and
Birmingham's ideals.

But you weren't
Neo-classical.
Or "iconic",
Apparently.
So the philistines
Pulled you
Down.
Brutal.

H.J. Wilkinson (17 1/2) after E.J. Thribb.

A Birmingham of the memory
by Stewart Lee

Though I grew up in the '60s and '70s just outside
Birmingham's south eastern edge, in Shirley and then
in Solihull, I inherited a Birmingham accent and a
Birmingham attitude from my family, relatively recent
transplants to the suburbs who'd drifted into Birmingham from rural Worcestershire at the turn of the 20th
century. They came to seek betterment in the City of
A Thousand Trades, carved out of nothing in an act
of will by the city fathers in the Industrial Revolution,
and found themselves mixing chocolate in Bournville,
welding cars in Northfield, and doing things in department stores on Corporation Street. But their relationship with Birmingham was complicated.

I remember my mother stifled her accent whenever
she was on the phone to strangers. And in 1972, I
noticed that my grandfather, a former Cadbury's
messenger boy who could recite old Black Country
music hall routines pitch perfect, eliminated his native
intonations entirely when interviewed by ATV news
about a neighbour's mysterious death, replacing them
with a strangely strangulated received pronunciation
the like of which I had never heard before, or since.
And when I started on the stand-up comedy circuit in
London in 1989 I too snuffed out the last traces of my
accent. Regional stand-up acts — the cheeky scally or
the brutal Glaswegian — were expected to say certain

things, to fulfil certain stereotypes, and I didn't want to be pigeonholed. The wind changed. My voice went. And I denied Birmingham as surely as Peter denied Christ.

I left in 1986 and everyone who held me to the city has now died or drifted away. My Birmingham is, by necessity, a Birmingham of the memory; a weekly bus ride with my gran over the rickety Digbeth flyover to hand the Place The Ball coupon into the Evening Mail offices; the four-year-old me marvelling before Nicholas Monro's King Kong statue in Manzoni Gardens, a significant sculpture typically disowned by the city; the psychedelic survival of a '60s clothes shop on New Street that looked like a cave carved out of alien ice; Father Christmas at Rackhams and The Wombles live at Bingley Hall; an illuminated Ansells advertisement by the Bull Ring of a beer glass that magically drained itself; '70s pantomimes starring great old-school comics, like Eli Woods or Rod Hull and Emu, and my mother asleep in her seat; my mother and I attending a then-exotic hindu wedding in a great silken canopy; my mother and I clearing the houses of a dozen dear departed aunties, their homes vertical graves in Dad's Lane and Raddlebarn Road and Alcester Lane's End; shops like Dungeons and Starships, Andromeda Books and the original subterranean subway site of Nostalgia And Comics, stinky gathering places for the faithful before nerd-chic rendered fandom sexy; Reddington's Rare Records at Moor St station, where the ignorant teenage me passed over now priceless and then unwanted Vertigo vinyl in favour of passing punk fads; listening to the Handsworth Riots on the police radio frequency and thinking about Steel Pulse; justifying a

charity grant to an attic full of Freemasons in Hale-
sowen every Christmas in the '80s; and adolescent
cultural epiphanies — The Fall and Ted Chipping-
ton at the Powerhaus, Dexy's Midnight Runners and
the comedian Peter Richardson at the Hippodrome,
UB40 at the Odeon when they were still brilliant, the
pre-Raphaelites and the performance artist Anthony
Howells at the Art Gallery, the Edward Burne-Jones
windows in the Cathedral, and all those jangly C86
bands at Burberries on the then-unreconstructed
Broad Street, in the last long August evenings of the
Summer I skipped town for good.

Unlike my Birmingham, the website Paradise Circus's Birmingham, as encapsulated by their book 101
Things Birmingham Gave The World, is not a Birmingham of the memory. It is a living breathing thing,
wrestling with the city's contradictions, press-ganging
the typically arch and understated humour of the
Brummie, and an army of little-known facts, both
trivial and monumental, into reshaping its confusing
reputation.

Paradise Circus's Birmingham is funny, profound,
innovative, historic, and blessed with both a sense of
its own absurdity, and a modest pride in its often un-
heralded achievements. Even the name of the website,
drawn from a fairly nondescript city thoroughfare,
embodies Birmingham's contradictions, its unbeaten
belief in better. For the teenage me, Jon Bounds's and
Jon Hickman's resource would have been a lifeline,
giving Birmingham the same secret and magical living
subtext Iain Sinclair has given to East London, Alan
Moore has given to Northampton, Tim Bradford has

given to Stoke Newington, and Francis Brett Young gave to the fictional village of Monk's Norton. For the adult me, it's an unadulterated pleasure.

The older I get, the more I think about the city that shaped me, and regret the things I didn't engage with.

I wish I'd seen Robert Lloyd's post-punk prophets The Nightingales first time around on home turf, rather than a decade later in London; I wish I'd known The Swell Maps lived at the end of my road; I wish I'd learned about the Birmingham surrealists and the Kardomah café and had done some digging; I wish I'd walked a self-mapped public sculpture trail of the works of William Bloye and read Shenstone while lying on the grass in the Leasowes; I wish I'd spent the summer I was 18 drinking exclusively in atmospheric city centre pubs now long gone, instead of in brightly lit Solihull boozers on faceless new build estates; I wish I'd got to know the diaspora of my ancestral Worcestershire émigrés better, spread out as they were like stars along the Western side of the city; and I wish I'd been to Barbarella's and The Boggery, to dance to The Dangerous Girls or laugh at Malcolm Stent.

But it's too late for all that now.

In exile, we make our peace with the past. My mother and her parents, despite deserting, are all now buried within the city bounds, the subject of sporadic pilgrimages. And my accent, well, it comes back, according to my wife, in moments of excitement, anger, passion, drunkenness, and hilarity, when genuine emotion breaks through a conscious attempt to suppress the real self. To me, it appears, the Birmingham accent is the voice of unvarnished truth. And I access the accent deliberately, on stage as a stand-up, whenever I channel nostalgic memories, or whenever I want to make a provocative idea sound just that little bit more reasonable. No-one is expecting cleverness or cunning in a Birmingham accent. But it is much wiser than it seems. And so is 101 Things Birmingham Gave The World. Forward!

Stewart Lee, writer-clown, Stoke Newington, London, October 2014

Contents

No. 1: HP Sauce

It's made in Holland and named after a London land-mark, so of course HP Sauce is the Brummiest thing going. It's "the best known brown sauce in the United Kingdom" and slavered across sausages the length of the land, despite brown sauce sounding more like a euphemism for, well, shit.

If that's not enough of a sauce based double-entendre for you, HP Sauce became known as 'Wilson's gravy' in the 1960s and '70s after Harold Wilson's wife revealed he "covered everything" with it. Lucky old Mrs Wilson.

What gives it its unique taste is tamarind, and when the Midlands Vinegar Company launched the sauce back at the turn of the last century it was in Aston. The vinegar was made on one side of the A38 and piped over the road — you couldn't get much more Brummie unless the tamarind pods were trod by Rustie Lee.

And then Heinz bought it and upped production sticks to the Netherlands, which to be fair sounds like a place brown sauce comes out of.

JB

No. 2: Nuclear War

Schoolchildren in the 1950s and '60s spent as much time learning how to 'duck and cover' in the event of a nuclear missile attack as they ever did about algebra and home economics. They grew up with a perpetual and very real fear that the Cold War would one day escalate into a mind-boggling violence played out on a global scale. Their own kids fared no better, exposed as they were to a seemingly out-of-control 1980s arms race that was, such was the fascination of the time, to be apparently conducted in outer-fucking-space.

These fears were constantly backed up with footage and accounts of the two atomic bombs dropped on Japan by Allied Forces at the end of World War II, on the cities of Hiroshima and Nagasaki, along with powerful (children's!) fiction such as Raymond Briggs's *When The Wind Blows*, and the still-terrifying-but-not-for-kids BBC drama, *Threads*.

Two generations of children, then, had a very clear understanding of how the world would eventually and inevitably end. It would end in a rain of fire, where dying instantly within the one-mile blast zone was infinitely preferable to surviving the explosion and then waiting for the sweet release of choking one's last breath, some weeks later, if you were very lucky, in a refugee camp riddled with the radiation pox and human shit.

None of this death, destruction, fear and creeping terror would have ever been possible without the city of Birmingham.

In the early '40s, at the city's University, Rudolph Peierls and Otto Robert Frisch developed a technique whereby uranium bombs could be constructed with a critical mass of only 6kg, which made them a viable airborne threat. This development lead directly to the creation of those deadly missiles dropped on Japan and to 40 years of enduring panic.

CH

No. 3: Manchester

Ah, Manchester! Competitive little Manchester! Gutsy, plucky, Manchester! What makes you tick? What makes you worry so much about Birmingham? What makes you enter into dick-measuring contests with us all the time? Well, our Psychology 101 training suggests it's something oedipal. Tell us, people of the North, tell us about your mother.

Folksy little Manchester was something of a 14th Century Etsy, producing all manner of cutesy home spun bits of Flemish weaving, that was of course until Birmingham started and then sent the Industrial Revolution up country to them, giving them the opportunity to step up their ideas a bit and start to grow.

While Birmingham, a sort of Cupertino for the 1700s, was busily producing more and more great ideas to set out into the world, Manchester rolled up its sleeves and swore it would be bigger than us one day, just you wait and see.

And so, like Frankenstein's Monster, it lurches about the place grasping at things it doesn't understand and crying out. One day its clumsy fists might crush Birmingham, the maker. We can't stop it and perversely we don't want to. We watch Manchester, simultaneously disgusted and fascinated by it as it shouts something about having more sausages than us, bellowing something about Salford.

Imagine the chip they'd have on their collective shoulders if they were Scousers.   *- JH*

No. 4: The Football League

Football has had a long and evolutionary history taking in local rivalries, struggle with authority, class warfare, co-option and paganism; but enough of St Andrews. Everything we know about football today originated on the other side of the city: from fixture congestion, to dead rubbers, from runaway leaders to mid-table obscurity, cynicism and playing for the draw.

All because the Villa's lushly bearded William McGregor was fed up with cup ties and friendlies and knocked football-admin heads together around the country and in 1888 instigated the Football League.

So we not only have him to thank for the spread of the sport across the week and the country, but also for professionalism. For without regular games there was no way to build crowds and make money. So Birmingham created and hence ruined the modern game. It created John Terry.

And in reality it created Post Vale versus Yeovil on a wet Tuesday night in November, not quite what he intended when he wrote: "clubs are compelled to take on teams who will not attract the public."

JB

No. 5: Pissing

This is one for the guys, ladies you might want to sit down. Remember when you were learning how to 'do a standing up wee'? The hardest thing was getting your little soldier to hit the target. Now then: what did you aim for? That's right! There was some writing near the back of the pan.

Now you probably couldn't read at that age, but very soon you could and one day you'd be having a jimmy and you'd finally decode that writing: 'Armitage Shanks'. From that day on you'd see those letters every time you went for slash for they are the motto to which we urinate. The connection between those words and relief is so strong that I often need to stop several times to spend a penny when I drive past road signs in Staffordshire.

But there wouldn't be an Armitage Shanks to shoot for if it wasn't for Birmingham. For it was here that two great sanitary giants met to thrash out a peace that led to the formation of Armitage Shanks in 1969. Yes here in Birmingham, the Switzerland of Pissing, Armitage Wares of Armitage agreed to merge with Glasgow's Shanks Holdings — and just as well for this writer would not be able to cope with the hilarity of piddling into toilets stamped 'Shanks Holdings' ('Yes! I am!').

So ladies — welcome back — the reason we never sprinkle when we tinkle is all thanks to Birmingham. And if our aim goes wrong don't worry — we'll be sweet and wipe the seat.   *- JH*

No. 6: New Zealand

For most of living memory New Zealand was simply a fictional village that was used to rehouse spent characters from *Neighbours*. In *Neighbours* — and by extension all popular culture of the 1980s and '90s — a trip to New Zealand was equivalent to the Eastenders trope of 'going up West': something other and exotic, but never seen.

All this was set to change when popular Birmingham pointy sword franchise The Lord of the Rings went to those sleepy antipodean islands in 2001. So popular was the film series that it single handedly regenerated New Zealand, taking this abstract idea of a place and fixing it in the minds of a generation of gap-year students: a backpacking destination was born.

Before Birmingham's intervention, the biggest cultural event to happen to New Zealand was the arrival of community radio DJ Henry Mitchell from Erinsborough.

No Birmingham, no New Zealand.

Imagine what David Lodge's Campus Trilogy could do for Samoa.

JH

No. 7: Cluedo

As Anthony Pratt and his family huddled in their King's Heath Anderson shelter while the Luftwaffe flew over Birmingham, it bothered him that there was nothing to do. He was concerned that, rather like Christmas, all you could do was sit in a confined space with your nearest and dearest and wait for the whole thing to blow over. Something was desperately needed to relieve the boredom. So he invented Cluedo. And, all over the world, Christmas was saved.

We're told that Birmingham City Council has refused to exploit Cluedo's tourism potential, or even acknowledge Cluedo as a product of Brum, as it claims it does not want the city to be associated with homicide. But it's a Brum thing alright, and is said to be based on nearby Highbury Hall.

Tony's neighbours had already invented Buccaneer (no, not Buccaroo, calm down at the back) and he wanted in on the act. He pitched his new board game to Waddingtons and they liked it. They made a few directorial changes and began mass production. It became one the most popular board games in the world.

Not that Balsall Heath-born Tone was able to enjoy the life of a millionaire. A bit short of financial advice, he signed over his royalty entitlements for a one-off payment of £5,000.

He died in 1994 in a nursing home.

In the Lounge.   - *SN*

No. 8: Charlie and the Chocolate Factory

Trap one in the gents at my work is always locked. No one ever goes in; no one ever comes out. I call it Willy Wonka's shithouse. To myself that is — it doesn't really come up much in conversation.

That, rather than the two films, the West End musical, or the use of 'Oompa Loompa' to describe the spray-tan aficionados on Broad Street, is how I know that Roald Dahl's *Charlie and the Chocolate Factory* is truly part of our popular consciousness.

Cadbury World, without ever explicitly saying so, plays on the ubiquitous idea of a chocolate factory being an exciting and magical place, staffed by smiling, singing and dancing workers in primary coloured uniforms. The real Cadbury workers will be in hairnets and white coats, worried for their jobs after the Kraft take-over, and unlikely to do much singing as there isn't a pub for miles. I've no idea what is in Cadbury World, the attraction, but chocolate rivers and sweet-laying geese are less likely than a moth-eaten tableau of Mr Cadbury's Parrot and some large sepia photos of Bournville looking pretty similar to how it does now.

A capitalist bait-and-switch on poor parents looking to fill the long dark half-term of the soul the place may be, but Birmingham has every right to trade on Charlie Bucket and co. For without Birmingham, there'd be no Cadbury's and without Cadbury's there'd be no *Charlie and the Chocolate Factory* in any medium.

When Roald Dahl was a pupil at Repton, the school was often sent new Cadbury products for the boys to try and the experience inspired the older Dahl to write a book about the fabulous place that these confections must have come from. Note that he'd never been to the factory, he made it all up: there is no chocolate river in Birmingham. Some of the canals have brown stuff floating in them, but it's not something you should eat.

Had Roald actually got on the number 11 and gone to Bournville, the book might have been very different: the golden tickets would have been 2-for-1 entry offer vouchers from the *Evening Mail* and the story would have ended not with the business being given to a deserving child but sold to an American conglomerate putting thousands of jobs at risk. Oh, and a chance to buy some misshapen creme eggs at a slightly reduced price.

As ever, the Birmingham of our imagination is the real winner.

JB

No. 9: Going to the Pictures

It's an incontrovertible yet nonetheless contested fact that Birmingham's Electric Cinema is the oldest working cinema in the UK. Birmingham can, then, claim an important part in the history of cinema in Britain. The Electric, though, is a peculiar beast. Those who would dismiss its claim to be an historic venue might point out that very little remains of the building of 1910, and so look instead look to the South East — to Brighton's Duke of York's or London's Phoenix (née the East Finchley Picturedome). Of course, it better suits the accepted narrative of arts and culture that such things would belong to the capital or its artistic dormitory town, so The Electric is easily brushed aside by historians and journalists.

In explaining to you how Birmingham invented going to the pictures I will also brush aside any mention of The Electric because going to The Electric is not, you see, going to the pictures.

The Electric has had many uses in its lifetime but has primarily had two incarnations: one as a smut house, and the other as an art house (which is often similar to smut but has better lighting and subtitles). It is more conventionally known for the latter and essentially trades as such today. The thing about The Electric, though, is that it is *not* a place where one goes to the pictures: it is a place where one demonstrates distinction when watching cinema releases. What do I mean by this? The Electric's thing is to be a little more expensive then the rest and by being so to promise you things you don't get down the multiplex: nice food, beer (brewed by a micro brewery just a few miles away *of course*), a decent selection of scotches, a big squishy sofa and beautiful hipster staff who bring you olives if you send them a text. It is categorically not what happens over at Rubery Great Park where you can buy nachos with plastic cheese and a 2 litre cup of pop from a (rightfully) angry minimum wage teenager in a gigantic '90s-built metal shed. That's for *other people*, we are better than that and we want to enjoy our film in the quiet THANK YOU VERY MUCH. The Electric does all of this whilst actually running like a mini-multiplex. For all of its art cinema posturing and pedigree it runs a programme of only the most bankable and accessible independent fare bolstered up by Marvel superhero franchises. In this regard The Electric and its clientèle can have their homemade organic carrot cake and eat it.

There is something about The Electric though, a certain glamour in the architecture within, that belongs to Birmingham and belongs to the story I need to tell you: how Birmingham invented going to the pictures.

What do I mean by going to the pictures? I mean cinema as a great democratised pastime, not the sort of middle class fussiness that goes on at The Electric today. Ironically, considering where we are now with the out-of-town multiplexes, it all did begin with a bit of glamour, a bit of glitz, which turned up on the Birchfield Road in Perry Barr.

It was here, in 1930, that Balsall Heath's Oscar Deutsch opened the very first Odeon cinema. The

Cinema Treasures history website describes the venue for us:

> The facade was painted white and had rounded features that gave an impression of domes. Inside the auditorium seating was arranged for 1,160 in the stalls and 478 in the balcony. An unusual feature was that the stalls area widened out towards the proscenium. There were Moorish scenes painted on the side walls in the front stalls area.

Now Oscar had already opened a less glamorous Black Country picture house but with the Perry Barr Odeon he perfected the model for his cinemas. He decide to stick with the name 'Odeon' and hired the building's architect, Henry Weedon, to design more of the same and then he rolled out his nascent chain to the rest of the country. Oscar had invented going to the pictures: a little bit of glamour and glitz, uniformed ushers, ice cream trays and intermissions, packets of Poppets or chews, an advert for a Chinese restaurant just a few hundred yards from this screen — it all started in Perry Barr.

Time moves on and over the years the model began to change. There's less of the glamour now then there was before because cinema has been moved out of those beautiful Art Deco buildings into vast pleasure domes on cheap land out of town. But for a while there Oscar had brought a little bit of stardust to us all. Yes, going to the pictures was a wonderful thing but now all I'm left with is misty eyed nostalgia about what we have lost that leaves me sounding like a Peter Kay routine. Do you remember those cartons of drink they had? With the spiky straw? Not Capri Sun, the others. You had to stab the straw through and if you got it wrong it would bounce off. And Nerds? Orange and green they were. Do you remember? Do you remember? Sweets? When you were a kid?

So what became of Oscar's dream? Well, other than a series of leveraged buy-outs and mergers that have remapped the network of cinemas and cinema chains, he left behind a lot of architecture. The smaller community cinemas of days gone, abandoned by the march of progress out to Star City and Rubery, left behind shells that needed to be filled. Such beautiful shells.

The fate of these buildings differs from place to place. In Asian neighbourhoods they have become banqueting suites, their mix of space and interior features making them perfect for weddings and special occasions. In poorer white neighbourhoods they are bingo halls, which turns out to be an even quicker way of taking folks' cash than the obscene markup on cinema hot dogs; meanwhile in the boho white areas, those places with an upswing of gentrification, they burn these palaces to the ground so that they can fit in more flats and indie coffee shops. For anyone else, they also make a good Wetherpoons. You can chart the changes in communities over time by the uses of their old cinemas which change as demographics swing. Indeed that first ever Odeon, on the Birchfield Road, has been a bingo hall and is now a banqueting suite. It's never caught fire but there was an awkward attempt to clear it by some Germans looking to spread their lebensraum in the 1940s — damage caused by their bombs led to the loss of much of the building's Art Deco exterior and it was rebuilt in a much more austere fashion. In many ways we invented not just going to the pictures, but what to do when the pictures have gone.

JH

No. 10: Gynaecology

"And when you gaze long into an abyss the abyss also gazes into you." Friedrich Nietzsche, *Beyond Good and Evil*

I can't speak for other social strata or areas, but in a working class home in Birmingham if you ever start a sentence "I'm not a…" dads in other rooms will bound over furniture and push small children out of the way to run in and say "I'm not a gynaecologist, but I'll have a look," and then walk away with a giant shit-eating grin.

As well they might if they knew of long time resident of Birmingham 'King of the Quim' Lawson Tait. Lawson is known for a few things: his strong anti-vivisection views, his demonstrating the link between cleanliness and mortality rates before the theory was generally accepted, but, maybe most famously, he is known as one of the fathers of modern gynaecology. Lawson, born Robert Lawson, is responsible for pioneering a bunch of lifesaving lady bits operations and kick-started a field of medicine that has kept women healthy 'down there' ever since. Any friend of the vulva is a friend of mine.

He was also responsible for the appendectomy, so if you ever had to have a few weeks off school and got to eat ice cream to recover, you have Lawson to thank. Wait, that could be tonsils? Who knows? I'm not an otolaryngologist… but I'll have a look

No, that doesn't work.   - *DS*

No. 11: The Sound of Silence

I've got something I need to tell you about Birmingham. It'll be legend…

— wait for it —

…dary.

I need to tell you about Birmingham and how it invented the dramatic pause. Well, the one they have on the telly anyway.

Rhetoricians have always known that the pause is a powerful thing: it's the white space of oratory design. Just as a graphic designer needs to balance harmony and discord to create, and then play, with tension on the page, so too the public speaker uses silence, the pause, as negative space to better punctuate their message.

In broadcasting one cannot be quiet. Radio folk talk of 'dead air' — silence in other words, a moment when no one is speaking, no music is playing, nothing is being advertised. The one thing a radio broadcaster can never have on their show is dead air because the moment that you are silent is the moment that you lose your audience. Dead air suggests that the receiver has lost signal from the broadcaster. Perhaps the radio needs to be retuned, or perhaps the station is off air — whatever it is it's time to touch that dial. On most stations there is an 'emergency tape' (copy of an M People record) that will kick in automatically should quiet pervade for too long.

When the BBC started to broadcast television, they essentially showed radio with pictures. The techniques of broadcasting had been shaped on the radio, and everyone who worked in television had worked on radio, so television was merely radio remediated with an extra quality: the picture. It took 70 years for the innovation that changed everything: it took 70 years for the invention of a broadcast silence.

It took Brummies, of course, to take the big risks and to bring about these changes: it took a Brummie mindset to realise that with a *picture* you could sustain a silence in your work because the audience could see that you were still there. This was intentional silence, not dead air: it took Brummies to bring the art of public speaking back to mass entertainment and they did that when they invented the silence.

I can tell you how they did it. I've got the answer here in my hand…

...but we don't want to give you that.

Will you read on, or take the answer? You're going to play!

Silence has enabled television to create new moments of tension. Silence has enabled television to tease and titillate the audience, tickling them somewhere special to hold them back for a few moments. I'll tell you all about it...

...after the break.

<u>End of Part 1</u>

Birmingham's place in the pantheon of advertising doesn't really come from the many things we've invented: by the time advertising became an artform, too many of our discoveries had become generic. Our big brands have never really played on their roots: unlike the way Apple uses California you can't exactly see Birmingham used as a stamp of quality or cool. Cadbury's honourable exception is the Bournville brand of plain chocolate, but you don't see Newey and Eyre using 'designed in Marston Green' on the packaging of lightbulbs. Even Baguette Du Monde pretends to be French.

No, we're more usually used to convey a particular type of enthusiastic gaucheness: "anything for you cupcake" says some chap in a hotel advert, "we wanna be tugethur" says Mark Williams. This would be worth further investigation were we not flummoxed by the appearance of Williams (also the 'running Brummie dad' in the Fast Show) into spending all of our time wondering why the main ginger kid in Harry Potter has a

London accent when all the rest of his family are clearly from Great Barr.

No, our main contribution to advertising seems to be dyslexic rude words, or other methods to get your attention by shock. Many tried to make punk work in advertising, but it took Balsall Heath's own hirsute Don Draper, Trevor Beattie to invent the FCUK T-shirt, and also the <u>ironic sexism</u> of the 'Hello Boys' Wonderbra ads.

Part 2

Before the break we were about to find out how Birmingham had invented the broadcast silence — the dramatic pause — and so changed the way we watch TV forever.

Well, you see it was *Who Wants To Be a Millionaire* that brought the silence to your television, and that international format comes from round here (not London as you might have thought). Produced by Celador, a company which had previously produced star vehicles for its Acock's Green-born founder Jasper Carrott, *Millionaire* was created by the current Don of the Shelbies: *Peaky Blinders* show-runner and Small Heathen, Steven Knight.

We should also mention that Chris Tarrant, the show's UK presenter, and the format's original and template host, is a powerhouse of Midlands broadcasting. After being educated at the University of Birmingham, Tarrant fronted local TV news here in the Second City before he found his true calling as a broadcasting innovator, a test pilot for his craft. Firstly he pushed the boundaries of children's television on Birmingham based *Tiswas*, then he moved on to front an adaptation of top Brummie board game <u>Cluedo</u> before finally realising his destiny as the strong silent type, the quizmaster of *Millionaire*.

Who Wants To Be a Millionaire set the tone for most post-millennial game shows: swooshing lights, chrome sets, but most of all the idea of a sadistic yet avuncular host who will just suddenly freeze and stare at contestants, unblinking, unmoving, and *unspeaking* leaving them to sweat in the stew of their own answers, their own fate, before leaping up to bear-hug them when the victory music sting crashes in and the lighting mood changes up to success. Then presumably it's all down to The Garrison Tavern for a pint. And we owe it all to Birmingham.

Shhhhhhhhhh!

JH (commercial breakdown by JB)

No. 12: Fannying About On A Yacht

When you pick up *Hello!* or flick to the most exploit-ative pages in the tabloids what are you likely to see? One may have upskirt pics of vulnerable young actresses, one may have charming stories where you get to see just what the kitchen looks like in the house Sienna Miller has hired for a photoshoot. But both will have long-lens pics of celebrities fannying about on a yacht.

Yes, whether they're oligarchs, sportspeople, singers, or simply government ministers enjoying the free hospitality, all famous people like to lay back on deck and sup cocktails. But back in the olden days, messing around in boats was done in the mode of people from Walsall like Jerome K Jerome: you had to row your-bloody-self, what good was that?

But in 1982, thankfully, Birmingham took the lead and the Taylors, Rhodes-y and sweet little tubby Simon Le Bon showed everyone how it was done in the video to Rio. No-one quite set the template for looking rich on a boat like the Durannies, and I'm sure it was their time spent in Saramoons that done it.

JB

No. 13: Radio 1

The 1960s, as we're often told, was a turbulent time. A time of sexual liberation, mind-expanding drugs and endless streams of footage of Twiggy walking down Carnaby Street, and George Best pouring sparkling wine into a pyramid of champagne glasses.

When talk turns to radio, however, the cameras always inevitably turn seawards, a bobbing sea trawler covered in radio masts, swiftly followed by fashionably dressed men staring earnestly at dials and switches, then wheeling their chairs over to pick another seven inch from the rack.

I am talking, of course, about pirate radio, and if you were a hip young thing in the early to mid 1960s, pirate radio was the only way you could listen to pop music over the airwaves. That is, until 1967 when, after pirate radio stations were outlawed by an act of parliament, the BBC split the Light Programme into two stations, BBC Radio 1 and BBC Radio 2, the former having a remit to play popular music.

Radio 1 sprang into life at 7:00am on 30 September 1967, with Tony Blackburn introducing the very first record, *Flowers in the Rain* by The Move, marking the beginning of the establishment's acceptance of post war rebellion, and the end of the '60s.

The Move were, as any fule kno, formed in Moseley in 1966, and the band have a strong Brummie pedigree. Vocalist Carl Wayne went on to star in Brummie wobbly soap *Crossroads* and lead guitarist Roy Wood later formed Wizzard (and enjoyed having his Christmas dinner at Walsall Rugby Club, though not every day). Bassist Chris 'Ace' Kefford was so cool, even the mighty Sabbath were in awe of him after catching a glimpse of him climbing out of a Rolls while they waited for the number 11 bus. Bev Bevan, drummer and Jasper Carrott's best man, was once told by Paul McCartney that he was a better drummer than Ringo Starr and rhythm guitarist Trevor Burton went on to form Birmingham supergroup Balls (no sniggering at the back there).

It's often said that the first step you take on a journey sets the tone for the rest of that trip: The Move, for all they were pop stars, were never properly *cool*, and Radio 1 would never really be either.

Who knows what journey Radio 1 could've taken if Tony Blackburn had picked *Massachusetts* by The Bee Gees (which turned out to be the second track he played) instead of The Move's opus.

Perhaps the airing of such a <u>middle-of-the-road</u> track would have set the station on the road to cosy conservativism, with Tony Blackburn's breakfast tenure lasting well into the mid-90s and a young John Major shockingly rising to power in 1979 instead of Margaret Thatcher. Or it could've gone the other way, a revitalised rebellion seeing John Peel doing drivetime, and dinner tables across the country being treated to The Fall in session every other Thursday, influencing a socialist revolution and Britain becoming a rock 'n' roll utopia.

This is of course all idle speculation, but one thing is certain, we can categorically state that the Tea Cosy's first choice of record gave a distinctly Brummie twang to a national institution.

SH

No. 14: Daily Mail Britain

Do you have a Facebook account? If you do, I'll bet that at some point in the last month or so you'll have read a mind-bendingly stupid, or downright offensive comment made by a vague acquaintance — someone you went to school with, perhaps, or a former colleague from that place where you once worked.

Try as you might, you can't really blame Facebook for this. Stupidity is an idea that pre-dates the digital age and is something that never really goes out of fashion. These days, however, stupid ideas can breed with unprecedented speed and efficiency, thanks largely to platforms such as Facebook, and the facepalm du jour in UK stupidity is the belief that certain of our fellow countrymen and women are robbing us blind.

The UK government has been waging a really effective war on this front since 'winning' the 2010 general election. They've introduced us to the concept of 'hard-working families', something with which many can identify. For those who struggle to identify, the government, and media outlets supportive of it, have kindly provided us with almost daily examples of the polar opposite: scroungers. No-one wants to identify with that, not when hard-working families is on the menu.

Scroungers, for those unaware, pump out kids at an alarming rate and expect YOU to pay for their education, health and welfare. The government has been so successful in peddling the thin end of this particular wedge that we're now so mad at scroungers (and foreigners, who are swarthy scroungers) that we're no longer going to stand for it. If all this was part of a wider, more sinister agenda, like the dismantling of the welfare state and the privatisation of the health service, you'd have to admire the planning and execution.

Anyway, it's a sorry state of affairs, make no mistake about it. We should be forced to take a bloody good look at ourselves. Here's a thing, though: none of this divisive bullshit would have been possible without the city of Birmingham.

It was here, on 20th April 1968, that Stetchford-born Conservative MP, Enoch Powell, gave a speech that became the benchmark and the blueprint for anyone wishing to spout dangerous claptrap at the weak-minded. In Enoch's case his audience was the General Meeting of the West Midlands Area Conservative Political Centre, which sounds like a very weak-minded public indeed. Facebook, incidentally, was several decades away from being invented.

Powell famously predicted that 'rivers of blood' would flow through the streets if immigration continued un-checked. It was powerful, evocative stuff, and it became the basis and justification for the opinions of racist shitheads for the next 20-odd years. In much the same way, the present-day rhetoric about scroungers and Eastern Europeans will reliably inform the people of Britain, hard-workers and scroungers alike, all the way to a Wonga.com-sponsored welfare state.

When that happens, remember to say, "Littlejohn was right, bab".   - *CH*

No. 15: The Hollow Promises, Lies, and Shattered Dreams of Fame and Stardom

> Yesterday I was happy to play
> For a penny or two a song
> Till a fellah in a black sedan
> Took a shine to my one-man-band
> He said, "We got plans for you, you'd never dream"

You're a Star, Carl Wayne's theme song for Birmingham-based television talent show *New Faces*, tells the story of art constrained by commerce, of authentic culture packaged by a star system. The narrator finds success of a sort, measured in his new possessions and receives acclaim from all around but his song is a confidence trick. The only positive emotion he has is in the first line, and is already linked to the past: "Yesterday I was happy to play".

Musically too this is dour stuff, its leaden rhythm is hidden by a sing-along hook in the chorus. This is a cathartic song. Such melancholia makes *You're a Star* a strange anthem for a show like *New Faces* that fetishises stardom, a show whose very MacGuffin is the pursuit of fame. Yet this is perhaps greatest trick of stardom, that it hides its shame in plain sight. Indeed *New Faces*' great rival, *Opportunity Knocks*, achieved much the same feat of doublethink with Kiki Dee's *Star*, which camouflages the lines "They can build you up / And they can break you down / With just the right words" behind the jauntiness in an almost Smithsian way.

Now you'll be forgiven for thinking I'm about to claim that Birmingham invented Saturday night television (it played a hand in that, of course). Possibly you suspect I'm going to say that *New Faces*, filmed firstly at the ATV Centre off Broad Street and then latterly at the Birmingham Hippodrome, was the first television talent show and therefore the precursor of the blockbuster global formats *X-Factor*, *Pop Idol* and, er, *Fame Academy*. Sadly not: *Opportunity Knocks* predates *New Faces* by many years.

Perhaps you think I will make the case for Birmingham inventing the light entertainment public vote, which is so ubiquitous in the modern talent show era? To be honest we bodged that one. The theatre audience at *New Faces* could vote live via push buttons wired to Marti Caine's 'Spaghetti Junction' scoreboard but the rest of us at home had to write in on a postcard to place our vote. Uncle Bob and his *Opportunity Knocks* lot responded to the postcard innovation with a telephone vote meaning that the London show could give results on the night while here in Birmingham we had to wait a week for the postal votes to be collated. In any case, these are all petty side issues compared to the real issue at hand: how Birmingham invented the whole sham that is fame itself.

I like to think of *You're a Star* and *Star* as folk tales, passed down among celebrities, to remind them of their place in the world, and to remind them of what needs to be done to escape their fates. These songs are also a warning to the rest of us about the true nature of fame and they have their root in Birmingham. It's no accident then that it was Birmingham that transmitted Carl Wayne's message to the world. For the city keeps reaching out to the world to tell it the terrible truth of fame, its hollow promises, its lies and the dreams that it likes to shatter. Witness for example Birmingham's Walk of Stars.

On paper the Walk of Stars is a celebration of the city's favourite sons and daughters, a testament to their talent and their art and to the city that bore them. In reality it's a rather dispiriting list of <u>middle-of-the-road</u> crowd pleasers — and a lot of them are actually from the Black Country. That's a slight exaggeration perhaps. It's great to see Joan Armatrading there, taking her rightful place alongside Beverly Knight. Malkit Singh is there and he is a truly global star (he's the biggest selling bhangra artist of all time) so perhaps David Bintley (the dancer, you've seen him) is too? The relatively recent induction of David Harewood seems a touch previous and to my eyes cynically timed: his sudden beatification happened during his supporting run on hit US drama *Homeland* (spoilers: his character is dead now) and doesn't seem to connect with his wider body of work which includes being the advertising face of London. The rest of the gang are your standard Brummie household names, many of whom have now retired to play golf in Coleshill and really I can't stress enough how many of them are from the Black Country.

The Walk is at the bottom of Broad Street, Birmingham's party street, the crappest part of the crappest street we have in town and a location where you can often hear people ask "Is that a new star? Or did someone stumble out of the Walkabout and throw up?". Is this glamour? No. But it is fame. It is stardom. Success in entertainment is being at the gloomy end of a shabby road lit up by gaudy lights and covered in sick (your own, someone else's, they can't dust for vomit). It's greasy takeaways, a skinful of booze, and too many bad drugs. Broad Street is absolutely the right place to put this thing if you want to expose the lie of fame. That is what Birmingham is doing, systematically.

A starker reminder yet of the hollow sham of fame comes in King's Heath where the locals decided upon their own parochial monument to stardom. The Kings Heath Walk of Fame commissioned just one star, for Toyah Wilcox, on the pavement outside of the former Ritz Ballroom. That star had to be dug up when the Ritz (by then reimagined as a Cash Converters), where The Beatles had once played, burned down — presumably to make room for another mixed-use development of flats and shops.

All of these interventions — the star walks and the folk songs — are there to remind us of a truth that was revealed long ago, with a story that starts, of course, in Birmingham.

You see stardom, super-stardom even, comes from the early years of Hollywood. Cinema audiences began to recognise certain actors as they appeared from one film to the next and then began to actively seek out more movies with the same actors. Studios responded to this by promoting the popular actors, giving them better, and bigger roles, and packaging them up for that now-starstruck audience. Narratives about the actors, about their lives, their loves, their hopes and dreams, became an important part of this packaging, this manufacturing of the actor as a star-commodity.

This all worked pretty well for the film studios until four big stars realised that they didn't actually need those studios to run the business for them, because they themselves were the business. This Gang of Four quit their studios to form their own company. Of course they wouldn't have been stars at all but for their creation by the same machine that they had set themselves against, but nonetheless it created a powerful story that the value in films lay with the artists, not the moneymen (in modern parlance this is known as 'doing a Radiohead'). Those four artists were Mary Pickford, Charlie Chaplin, Douglas Fairbanks, and name director D. W. Griffith. The studio they created to represent their creative work was called United Artists, and within it they would have creative control over their own work (and a heck of a lot more profit).

The formation of United Artists revealed the dirty secret of the star system for the first time. Stardom was supposed to link to glamour and riches, obtaining fame was supposed to reify the American Dream, and yet here four of the fame's most privileged scions were recasting themselves as mere labour, as indentured (but well paid) servants.

Oh, and by the way it turns out that one of those artists was from Birmingham.

Charlie Chaplin had always claimed to be from London but over the past few years evidence has come to light that places his birth "on the 'Black Patch' near Birmingham". Chaplin, it's been claimed, may have been tightly managing his backstory, creating the perfect myth he needed to construct himself as a star, changing the parts that didn't suit. And he did become the perfect star, and with his United Artists colleagues he created a new form of stardom, a more empowered star with executive control. We can draw a direct line from Birmingham via Chaplin to Tom Cruise, who took on the running of United Artists himself in 2006. In Cruise, as with Chaplin, we have a bankable star very much in control of his own narrative, astute at managing perceptions and crucially in control of the money as well as being the public face of the work.

But we should remember that the star-capitalist, the actor who is also the owner of the means of movie production, is a rare beast indeed and for every Cruise or Chaplin there are hundreds of worker-actors, and for each of those there are thousands still whose dreams are trampled entirely. This is the world that Chaplin and the United Artists revealed to us. The worker-stars sing to themselves about this world in their folk songs, subversive messages to one another, warnings about the machinery of their fame. That's what Carl Wayne was doing each week on *New Faces* — reminding us of the truth that Chaplin had revealed.

Yesterday I was happy to play
For a penny or two a song
Till a fellah in a black sedan
Took a shine to my one-man-band
He said, "We got plans for you, you'd never dream"

And of course that 'Black Patch' wasn't even in Birmingham and it turns out that Chaplin was actually from the Black Country. It's just another lie, another piece of empty myth-making but it all fits. Let's get Charlie a star on Broad Street, just outside the Walkabout.

JH

No. 16: Karaoke

"Sing, Lofty," said Sgt. Major Tudor 'Shut Up' Williams, and Lofty did — tubby little everyman though he was. And tubby little everymen and everywomen around the world have sung too. Along to backing tracks, badly, when they've had just over the recommended amount of booze.

The recommended amount of booze being just a sip below the amount that assures you that other people need your version of *Paradise By The Dashboard Light* in their ears.

But, hang on, isn't karaoke a Japanese invention, like the digital watch and cartoon porn?

Well… back in the mists of computer and video time, Aston Micro-Electronics Ltd invented an easy way of putting captions on video. Electronically. Before that, karaoke would just be some sod reading the words to songs off a bit of paper. Aston dominated TV captions from their introduction in the 1980s. Indeed, for many in the industry, any TV word caption is an 'Aston', just as any vacuum cleaner is a 'Hoover' or any cola is a 'Coke' ("is Pepsi okay?").

And why were Astons called Astons? After Mr Aston? Hell, no. Aston in Birmingham of course.

So a world of slightly off-tune versions of things that have been done before was born. Just ask the *Evening Mail*.   *- JB*

No. 17: England's 1966 World Cup Triumph

48 years of hurst and counting. On that glorious summer afternoon, 30 July 1966, the sun shone on the British Empire for perhaps the last time. Kenneth Wolstenholme, Alf Garnett, future Birmingham City Manager Alf Ramsey and Jimmy Greaves were all at the apex of their happiness and, together, they ushered in an age of self-referential Aquarius. But would they have done it without the city of Birmingham?

Of course not.

It wasn't Sir Alf's premonition of him managing the blues that did it, nor was it Villa Park hosting West Germany's group games and the players possibly drinking too much at the Reservoir Ballroom in Ladywood. It wasn't even that the whistles blown by the referees were Birmingham-made.

We won because of the nation's belief that it was really possible. We won because Mr Ramsey said we would. Mr Ramsey said we would, not because he really needed to to audition for the top job at St Andrews, but because he believed anything was possible.

And anything was possible because of one black and white collie: Pickles who found the Jules Rimet trophy after it had been stolen before the tournament. And was that perky pup from Birmingham? No.

But it couldn't have been found if it hadn't have been

taken. And it couldn't have been taken if it wasn't at Westminster Central Hall (not in Birmingham) for the Stanley Gibbons (not from Birmingham) Company's Stampex exhibition. Thieves bypassed the millions of pounds worth of stamps, which were being heavily guarded, to half-inch the trophy, which wasn't. They wouldn't have had the idea for the heist had Brummies not been there first — pinching the original FA Cup from William Shillcock the jewellers in Newtown Row. But we can't claim that, that's way too tenuous.

You see, there isn't a stamp exhibition if there aren't stamps to exhibit. And there would be no stamps at all if it wasn't for Birmingham.

After inventing <u>the post</u>, in Birmingham, Sir Rowland Hill was working out how to make sure people could use it — he came up with the Penny Black, the first stamp.

Invention, exhibition, theft, dog, happiness, triumph, ennui — it's the way we can trail our history and identity, and Birmingham is the lickable, stickable, basis for it all.

JB

No. 18: Text Speak

The SMS is over twenty years old — and still no one has managed to come up with a past participle that sounds right when spoken. In a kind of way, the 'shortness' in the 'short message service' helped get us all ready for the brevity of Twitter, it's great for passing notes in class, and texting is a fantastic way to send news to people you don't really want to talk to right now.

But the 'shortness' was a problem, and wrestling with either ABC over the 2 key or Nokia's Stalinist rewriting of intent that was T9 didn't help. So luckily a group of lads from the West Midlands had invented a passable form of abbreviated written communications that was perfect.

In the early '70s a gang of prescient glam rockers from Walsall and Wolverhampton released a string of hit singles, delighted glitter-covered brickies everywhere, and foreshadowed a linguistic revolution. *Cuz I Love You*, *Look Wot You Dun* — you can see the spelling that you started to use on your mobile phone in the '80s evolve across Top of The Pops.

Yes, Slade invented text speak, and started its march to become lots of crappy little books sold by the tills in Waterstones, the sort you buy people for Christmas when you don't know them or like them very much.

And Walsall and Wolverhampton they may be from, but Slade were in the wider Brummie music scene, they couldn't have done it without the clubs and the people here. And, like many other people from the Black County they have stars on the Broad St Walk of <u>Fame</u>. So there.

JB

No. 19: British Satire

As Philip Larkin said about sex, British satire began in the 1960s and it has never looked back. *That Was The Week That Was*, *Beyond The Fringe*, Harold Macmillan impressions and that time when the varying heights of John Cleese and the Two Ronnies taught us all about class. Life was changing: young upstarts with just a public school and Oxbridge education behind them were bravely taking on the ruling elites that they were born to join and things would never be the same again.

But where would British satire be without the Cambridge University Footlights Dramatic Club, the comedy hothouse that produced Douglas Adams, John Cleese, Graham Chapman, Stephen Fry and, erm, Tim Brooke-Taylor? Displaying all the quiet entitlement of a cat lounging on clean washing, Footlights alumni have inhabited every matey TV panel show and chortlesome Radio 4 smug-in for four decades. And where would Footlights be without that distinctive name? Possibly just a footnote in history: another boring revue club, like they have at that 'other' university. And without Birmingham we would not have footlights.

In the late 1790s William Murdoch started experimenting with using the flammable nature of gas to provide illumination. He was a Scotsman who worked in Birmingham for Boulton and Watt at their Soho Foundry. By 1802 he'd devised a way to light the Soho factory and had even used gas to light his home, which suggests that Mrs Murdoch was either possessed of an admirable faith in her husband or some really high calibre insurance.

In 1808, Murdoch presented a paper to the Royal Society called *Account of the Application of Gas from Coal to Economical Purposes* for which he was awarded Count Rumford's gold medal, and the age of gas lighting arrived. Just three years later Westminster Bridge became the first to be lit by gaslight and it was followed by factories, streets and, of course, theatres.

Before Murdoch's invention, theatres were lit by guttering candle light, with the actors desperately shouting and mugging in heavy makeup to gain the audience's attention, often losing out to the action in the auditorium. Those in the posh boxes were usually OK, they could see the stage, wouldn't get their pockets picked and very rarely got torched by the candles. But for the poorer theatre-goers, taking in a show pre-gaslight could be hazardous.

Lamps using gas, which later would be refined with lime to create dazzling beams (your moment in the limelight, anyone?) transformed 19th century theatres. They went from places of garish rowdiness to scenes of youthful artiness and exploration, and became more inclusive and safer for the hoi polloi too. Albeit with just the tiniest risk of detonation if it all went wrong with that lime.

And over in Cambridge things were changing too. The university drama club had habitually performed elitist plays to elitist audiences, but in 1883, a group of Cantabridgians decided to create a new type of drama club, one that would appeal to the town as well as the gown, and they chose Footlights as their name.

History has failed to record whether the inaugural Footlights performance contained Gladstone impressions, an undergraduate dressed as Queen Victoria or a joke about Otto von Bismarck, but as 1883 was the year that Gaudi got cracking on the Sagrada Família, let's hope that there was at least one gag about unreliable builders. "This cathedral will definitely be nearly finished by the turn of the century, but I can't be sure which one — I've got a few other big jobs on first."

So, we can thank Birmingham and gaslight for the 1960s satire boom. And peachy-skinned young Emmas and Stephens have been taking pot shots at the ruling classes ever since, keeping them quaking in their hand-made Italian kidskin moccasins. And thanks to their incisive wit, wielded so ferociously on Radio 4 or in Richard Curtis films, the whole elitist house of cards has been brought crumbling down, so that never again will we be ruled by an in-bred class of overfed Etonian bully-boys. God bless you Birmingham.

LHB

No. 20: Photocopying your Arse

1779: James Watt patents a copying press or 'letter copying machine' to deal with the mass of paper work at his business. Luckily he also invents an ink to work with it. This is the first widely used copy machine for offices and is a commercial success, being used for over a century. This letter copying press is considered to be the original photocopier.

1779 Dec 15th: At the Lunar Society Xmas party, Matthew Boulton was seen removing his britches in the vicinity of the machine.

Only one of those statements is recorded in the history books, but we're saying both are definitely true.

JB

No. 21: The Global Economic Crisis

Are you troubled by debts, mortgage repayments, or other loans? Do you struggle to make ends meet? Are you tempted by those adverts on television offering short-term loans at rates of interest that would make a Serbian gangster blush?

If you are, then you are far from alone. People everywhere are feeling the pinch as the worldwide financial crisis lumbers on, sucking the hopes and dreams of tens of millions of human beings, right down the toilet. The blame for this mess has been laid firmly at the door of the banking community, and, to a lesser extent, those who draw their curtains during the daytime. For years, bankers the world over had been selling imaginary money to each other and pocketing the very real profits. When the bubble eventually and spectacularly burst, it was with such ferocity that the children's children of ordinary folk like you will still be paying for it when they are old and grey.

No, I don't really understand how it works, either, but it's bad. Real bad. Anyway. None of this huge mess would have been possible without the city of Birmingham, for it was here, in 1775, that Richard Ketley founded the world's first building society. Both Lloyds and Midland (now HSBC) Banks were also formed here shortly afterwards.

From its humble beginnings in the taverns and coffeehouses around the Snow Hill district of central

Birmingham, banking quickly became a very popular thing indeed, spreading globally within a matter of years, and eventually leading to the arsing financial meltdown we are all enjoying today.

We're all in this together, bab.

CH

No. 22: Hollywood

No, not Hollywood up by the Maypole. The real one of blockbusters and stars rather than Blockbuster and burnt-out cars. Because without a certain city not very far away you'd not be watching George Clooney gurn with his chest out, nor would you be able to grin through gritted teeth at the antics of those Forty Year Old Hangover chaps with the comedy.

We'd have missed the <u>stars and the studio system</u>, had to put up with only *On The Buses* between Ealing and *Love…Actually*. Or watched things with subtitles, confused as to exactly what all of the smoking men were mumbling about.

Because, movies are made of film, and film is made of celluloid. Which was a revolutionary new type of thing called a thermoplastic, first created as Parkesine in 1862 by Alexander Parkes in, yes you've guessed it, Birmingham.

JB

No. 23: The Internet

We are under attack. Our very way of life is threatened. All because of the fucking Internet. Make no mistake, we are at war with the machines now, today. It's already started. And there's one sure fire way to stop a war: **KILL HITLER.**

The Internet is the biggest problem we've ever faced. Systematically it has killed the record industry and the newspapers, it has made men look at more pictures of boobs and it has killed conversation. We need to stop it, but we can't, it's too late. To stop the decline of everything we hold dear we'd need to go back in time to before this all started. We'd need to kill Hitler. But who is Hitler in this Nazi analogy? And where would we need to go to stop him?

The best way to kill Hitler, or John Connor for that matter, is to go back in time and to stop him from even being born. The Terminator had a hard time tracking down John Connor's parents because most human records had been destroyed in the nuclear war between man and machines: the T-101 had to tear around California killing every Sarah Connor in the LA phone book systematically, going door-to-door in his search and even heading into town for a disco dance-off with the final target and her bodyguard. Fortunately for us we can turn the Internet upon itself. Using desk based guerrilla warfare we can seize the medium of our very oppression and we can track down the ground zero of the Internet revolution.

Ground zero is in Birmingham, UK.

So what's the plan exactly? We're not going to stop the Internet, but we're going to stop the bit of it that you always confuse in your head with it. We're going to stop the World Wide Web, which is the important bit, the bit that popularised using the Internet. Unless you're an American watching the Olympics Opening Ceremony, (in which case: "G'day Sport!") you probably know who Tim Berners-Lee is (American friends: he invented the World Wide Web which for your purposes means the Internet). But did you know that TBL is a Brummie? Oh yes, my friends, oh yes indeed.

Born in 1955 to glamorous computer science power couple Conway Berners-Lee and Mary Lee Woods, both of Birmingham, Brum's own Sir Tim is our primary target. Stop Conway and Mary from meeting, you stop Tim from being born and you save the world. But how will we do it?

Well, despite Hitler's best efforts, Conway had a good war during which the armed forces turned him into a ruthless high functioning mathematician and computer programmer. Mary's life took a similar course, being pushed through an accelerated learning programme and packed off to Malvern to do things with computers. It was this training, forged in blood, that led to them finally meeting and working together in their post-war lives (in Manchester, of all places). I can only imagine what growing up in a house full of computing knowledge did to corrupt young Tim's mind, and to set him on the wrong path. This all leads me to one conclusion: let's kill Hitler.

JH

No. 24: Thomas the Tank Engine

Railway enthusiasts get a bad press. If it's not the anoraks, glasses, and spots it's the destruction of the Tory countryside in order to build train lines. Or it's because they are Michael Portillo. Or it's — in the words of Daniel Kitson — that they "aren't paedophiles [they] just like the look". The clergy get a bit of that too. For all their overall historical good works, you might want to keep your nippers away from the Catholic ones.

Luckily, this particular tale of Brummie greatness features an Anglican cleric and 'railway enthusiast' who did something brilliant for kids: Wilbert Vere Awdry, better known as the Reverend W. Awdry who invented Thomas the Tank Engine.

In 1940 he became curate of St. Nicholas' Church, King's Norton, Birmingham and it was there in 1943 that he invented the characters that would make him famous — to amuse his son Christopher during a bout of measles. The rest is <u>Beatle</u>-flecked history.

It's disappointing to me at least that Birmingham-based fictional tourism isn't a little more Sodor and a little less Mordor. Although you can imagine orcs and hobbits and stuff starting their epic journeys at King's Norton station more easily than a public transport system that actually works.

JB

No. 25: Christmas

Chestnuts roasting on an open fire, Santa Claus on his sleigh, people moaning about how it all starts too early and has got all commercialised and stuff, I know it's been said many times, many ways, but Merry Christmas to you.

Most of our notions of modern Christmas come from the Victorian author Charles Dickens who, being the rock star of his time, toured the country reading from *A Christmas Carol*. Turning a then barely-noticed mark on the calendar into the jolly family-oriented affair we associate today.

He really saw the value of a time of year when we take time to connect with family and give out nothing but love. The story of Scrooge is ultimately one of redemption, not one of spiritual redemption but one of redemption through the forgiveness of others and connection with his family. The place where Chucky D chose in 1853 to first read from this book? Birmingham Town Hall, So really Birmingham is Christmas's Bethlehem.

Happy Holidays. And unless you're reading this in between 20 December and 6 January, yes we know we're too early.

JB with DS

No. 26: Calls Being Monitored for Training Purposes

The last time you had a right row with someone at your bank (maybe you'd changed address with them but they hadn't updated the one on your credit card) or you had to sit on hold to an ISP (because they hadn't properly cancelled the account you had before you moved, and they wouldn't talk to you as you hadn't phoned from the number they'd cut off), thank the city of Birmingham. For without the second city you'd have had to pop into an office to do it.

In 1965 the Birmingham Post and Mail installed the GEC PABX 4 ACD, which is the earliest example of a call centre in the UK, probably to deal with a huge influx of members to the Chipper Club. So, Birmingham gave the world: hold music, pressing '2' to speak to the billing department, recording calls for training purposes (but not so they can remember what they've told you) and labyrinthine telephonic 'customer service'. Thank you, Birmingham.

What Birmingham didn't give the world, it turns out was The Chipper Club: oh poorly rendered Fred Basset-lite of our collective childhood, why didn't you tell us you were unfaithful? With Portsmouth, and Hartlepool of all places. How many more?

JB

No. 27: Batman

"I'm the goddamn Batman"

Jim Lee: *All Star Batman & Robin, the Boy Wonder no.1*

Why claim Batman?

Birmingham isn't short of its own, real, superheroes after all. The Statesman is a Bromsgrove bank clerk by day and at night prowls the city in mask and ever-so-slightly too tight T-shirt ready to thwart drunks and burglars. Malala Yousafzai is a symbol of peace and hope all over the world with a seeming immunity to bullets. And Birmingham's Lunar Society were a team-up of some of the country's greatest free thinkers, geniuses, and crusaders for equality.

So, why claim Batman?

For a start, there's the fact that, for many, Alfred Pennyworth, Batman's loyal butler, confidante and father figure, will always be Northfield actor, Alan Napier. In tribute to his work on all 111 episodes of the wonderfully camp TV series the Joker's name in the 1989 Tim Burton movie was 'Jack Napier'. Of course, if Alfred was from Northfield in the DC universe some of the events wouldn't have gone quite as dramatically.

"Sir, a Mr Bane to see you"

"Thank you Alfred, time to face my nemesis, the man who has sworn to break me."

"No need, sir."

"What?"

"I murked him while he wasn't looking with a
steering lock that I keep by the door."

But I think Birmingham and Batman are intrinsically
linked. Not just in the literal sense that Birmingham
residents, John McCrea and Phil Winsdale, have
helped shaped Batman by being artists for DC. Or
even in the vague sense that Batman is a product of
the modern world, a world that Birmingham built.
After seeing his parents shot outside of a cinema a
young billionaire vows a war on crime blah blah blah.
A Birmingham man invented celluloid which made
cinema possible, we refined and developed the gun to
the point where it was mass produced with ease, and
where would Batman be without the Batmobile? Four-
wheeled cars were developed and tested in Birmingham.

Bruce Wayne can only afford to be Batman because he
inherited Wayne Industries and the fortune attached.
Wayne Industries makes pretty much everything and
its fortunes are rooted in Gotham's economy so deeply
that it could be argued that Batman would do more
good if he dedicated his life to growing his interests
in Gotham and working to eradicate unemployment.
Batman seems to be the idea of 'caring capitalism'
made flesh.

Batman's world is Gotham: a heavily industrialised city
somewhere in America. It's a world of abandoned fac-

tories, sleazy speakeasies, and high gothic architecture. His very essence depends on this noir look and feel, the disparity between the rich and poor, the shadows and alleys that make up a city half in decline. He just looks stupid on brightly lit streets, his mystique shrivels on a sunny day. Gotham is supposedly based on New York and got its name from the nickname given to New York by one-time Birmingham resident Washington Irving after the Midlands town. But it's a different New York to the one that's there now. Gotham may be the New York of old, but its docks are peppered with warehouses full of smuggled goods not hyper-vigilant NSA agents, its old industrial areas haven't been renovated into niche nightclubs and studio apartments, and the city has all the rough edges and problems any industrial city has.

Many of Batman's villains are not only products of an industrial city, but manifestations of the problems and challenges of living in them. The Penguin is the other, more real side of 'caring capitalism', aping 1930s 'high society' dress, he is the upper classes who establish and rule the city, exploiting its workers in unsafe factories without a care.

Mr Freeze — despite the pun-laden peak of Arnold Schwarzenegger's career — is actually a sad story: stealing diamonds as to keep his cryogenically frozen wife alive, Mr Freeze represents the conflict of commercial research and development. When the only goal is profit, human lives are not necessarily the focus.

One time public prosecutor Harvey Dent becomes Two-Face after an attack using sulphuric acid, (made in large quantities thanks to a lead chamber process developed, in Birmingham, by John Roebuck). Now with a split personality, Two-Face makes monstrous decisions at the flip of a coin (modern coin production established by Matthew Boulton in a plant, in Birmingham). Two-Face stands for the systemic failure and increasing corruption of bureaucracy. He exemplifies distrust of authority figures, never knowing when, if, or how the people that are supposed to be looking after them will turn bad.

Imagine Catwoman, and I bet you're imagining black patent leather. Invented in Birmingham by "A gentleman of the name of Hand" in 1793. Catwoman has been many things: thief, madame, femme fatale, hero, anti hero, and dominatrix to name but a few. In fact, as the western industrialised world's attitudes have changed about women in general, Catwoman has been there to challenge them. Including a brief period in 1954 where the Comics Code Authority strictly controlled the portrayal and development of female characters.

Batman the physical philanthropist, the caring capitalist, the captain of industry not only tackles these problems, but works to solve them, never resorting to murder. A man, not necessarily of the people, but for the people. Not really a man though, a ghost of industry, a figure haunting and guiding the industrial city's landscape. A landscape that is quintessentially Birmingham. When England dreams and feels its beating industrial heart, Birmingham is what it dreams.

Batman is Birmingham's patron saint.   - *DS*

No. 28: Analysing the Class Struggle

Nancy Mitford was a terrible snob. In a letter to Evelyn Waugh, she mentions with glee a mutual friend who uses the expression "rather milk in first" to express condemnation of those lower down the social scale.

In an essay for *Encounter* magazine, called *The English Aristocracy*, she listed a glossary of terms used by the upper classes along with the equivalents used by those who, to paraphrase Noel Coward, thought that television was for watching rather than appearing on. In doing so, she unleashed a wave of nose-looking-down directed at anyone caught saying 'settee' instead of 'sofa', or 'perfume' rather than 'scent'.

Yes, Nancy Mitford not only needed to check her privilege, but even created a ready reckoner with which to do it.

Nancy Mitford was a terrible snob, but at least she wasn't a Nazi. Nor did she come up with the idea of using a list of shibboleths to separate the English upper classes from those that would desire to emulate them. The groundwork, the idea of using synonyms rather than accents as class indicators, was done by Alan S. C. Ross, linguistics professor at the University of Birmingham and inventor of the terms U and non-U.

In 1954, Ross published a paper in a Finnish journal on 'the terminology of popular discourse of social dialects in Britain'. But it certainly didn't cause the stir that Nancy Mitford's use of his ideas did, just a few months later. Proof that it is indeed who (whom?) you know rather than what you know.

Birmingham, home of really understanding the class struggle: sweet. I mean, 'pudding'.

JB

No. 29: Heavy Metal

When Africans arrived in America as slaves during the 17th century, they brought with them a five-note musical scale that had evolved over centuries along the trade routes between Africa and the Middle East. Upon encountering the slightly different musical scale that the plantation owners had brought over from Europe, the Africans found that not all notes could be easily resolved. This led to a certain amount of improvisation and bending of strings that eventually resulted in what became known as 'blue' notes. These became the distinctive characteristics of wholly new African-American forms of music such as jazz and blues.

Stick jazz and blues, and its derivations such as R&B, together with the European folk music that had morphed into another truly American art form, country, and you eventually get rock and roll. It's a bit more complicated than that, but you get the picture.

The point is here that the movement of people — and the mixture of cultures and of music styles that go with it — is at the very heart of what makes pop music tick and what allows it to continually evolve. There are now more genres than you can possibly imagine, and that list will grow, and grow, as each new style eventually fractures into ever more complicated configurations of sub-genre.

In the late 1960s, lots of people wanted to be The Beatles, and it was easy to understand why. They were internationally famous and, along with a few other luminaries, seemed to be reinventing what pop music could be on an almost weekly basis. The main trouble with wanting to be <u>The Beatles</u> was (and still is) that, unless you grew up in the exact same circumstances, time and place as John, Paul, George and Ringo, and experienced the same things they had, then you were never going to be The Beatles: you were going to be something else entirely.

Four kids growing up in Aston, Birmingham, in the late 1960s liked The Beatles just as much as everyone else did. They formed a band. The trouble was, just as peace and love was giving way to the darker times of the 1970s, Aston (and Birmingham, generally) was not a place where you walked with flowers in your hair. Ansells Mild, maybe.

The result, as anyone who hasn't been living under a rock for the last 40 years will know, was a band called Black Sabbath, and they invented HEAVY METAL.

Genetically speaking, heavy metal is one of the stronger and more virulent of the musical genres to have evolved out of the actions of Dutch slave-trading bastards in the 1600s. And, like the Sabbath themselves, it is still going strong today, although it's morphed into a huge variety of sub-genres that are played and celebrated by millions the world over. In fact, the number of bands that have followed in the footsteps of Black Sabbath must surely by now rival those who have attempted to walk in even the Fab Four's shoes.

Granted, in some places, like Scandinavia, it can go a bit wonky from time-to-time and lead to the burning down of churches, or the occasional murder of a band member, but, by and large, metal is a Birmingham invention that truly did make the world a better place. The Dutch, incidentally, went on to give the world Golden Earring, The Vengaboys, and 2 Unlimited.

CH

No. 30: Tennis

Ever climbed Murray mount, "come on Tim", or knocked a sponge ball against a wall while grunting? Then you have Birmingham to thank for the gift of the only sport that doubles the price of a certain fruit for two weeks every year. Yes, Cliff Richards' favourite game was invented not in the white trousered environs of the Wimbledon croquet club, but up a back street in Edgbaston not a high lob from the old Firebird pub.

The rules of modern lawn tennis were drawn up, in 1859, by Harry Gem and his friend Augurio Perera who developed a game that combined elements of rackets and the Basque ball game pelota. The rest is, for the English at least, a posh and annually disappointing story.

Ace.

JB

No. 31: Class Conflict in Popular Culture

In 1908 26 men lost their lives just on the edge of Birmingham, but also on the edge of our understanding of the earth itself. Opened in 1876 Hamstead Colliery was at that point the deepest mine in the world — 2000 feet down beneath the surface. Not too far from where the Aldi is now.

At this point Birmingham led the globe in the technology of digging holes in the ground, the heroic deeds of those that went down them created stories and songs and flooded popular cognition: along with fishermen, miners were the working class cultural heroes that built a nation. These miners would be the foundation of the celebration of the differences between the rich and the poor — which is the central tension in all great Great British culture.

The high point — celebrating but diametrically opposite to the deep seam miners — is 1962's *Hole in the Ground* by Bernard Cribbins, which peaked at number nine in the charts. The numerologists amongst you will have spotted that there's a nine in 1908, and also that $1+0+8=9$ (much like how 1962's $1+6+2=9$) — that's no co-incidence. 54 years later ($54/9=6$, turn that around much like the miners and Cribbins were opposite terraneally, and they were both opposed to the ruling class and you get: a 9) Cribbins punished the capitalists, puncturing them with the sharp end of his spade. He dug it round when they wanted it square, he dug it where he wanted it to be: but most of all he dug it towards those class martyrs of Hamstead in Birmingham.

Noël Coward chose the record as one of his Desert Island Discs, probably unaware of the implied class genocide in the last verse. *Hole in the Ground* is one piece of popular culture where the working man comes out on top — literally — and that's a tribute to those that we lost. It's a tribute to the courage — and digging skills — of the men of Birmingham. Together they produced a message to the capitalists — and that's that.

JB

No. 32: The Post

Imagine a time before always-on instant communication with everybody. Imagine a world where you had to add your seal to a document in hot wax and have a messenger run it to its recipient. By the time they got there, no-one would care just how lovely the fucking cupcake you were eating was.

That's why we needed the post: reliable, accessible communication that was open to all, across the country and for a reasonable price. And it was all but invented by a chap from a suburb of a city not all that far away from us now.

Without the post, no *Night Mail*, Birmingham's W.H.Auden's best work. The phrases 'special delivery' and 'emptying sack' are also a godsend for smut merchants worldwide, and who do we have to thank? Sir Rowland Hill, who was a schoolteacher in Edgbaston mates with Joseph Priestley and Tom Paine, wrote a pamphlet entitled *Post Office Reform its Importance and Practicability*. The report called for "low and uniform rates" according to weight, rather than distance and pre-payment by the sender.

The dude later went on to lower train fares, for that too we'd like to lick his reverse side.

JB

No. 33: Daytime TV

The essential ingredients of daytime television are: jumpers, middle-aged people, chat. Whether they're hunting for antiques, buying or selling, or failing to sell things (especially houses), or even solving murders, or being real in some sort of institution — it's the middle-aged jumper chat that's important.

Once all that was on the day was programmes for <u>schools</u>, which would be shown by teachers happy to have a <u>cup of tea and a sit down</u>. In my class we counted down the clock until Fred Harris appeared, tidily bearded, did some sciencey thing and then went away again. At home, you did the dusting to the test-card music: praying for pages from Ceefax to brighten up the long dark teatime of the soul.

But then daytime TV arrived, and arrived live from the foyer of the BBC's studios in Pebble Mill. In Birmingham. It arrived with the middle-aged jumper chat formula already immaculately sorted. It was perfect daytime material, an audience in the studio that perfectly reflected the bewilderment of the viewer that any of it could be produced. It dropped uncomfortable pop stars on uncomfortable sofas, but managed to chivvy them all along whatever the adversity — Pebble Mill was in some ways the Scout Master of telly shows. Even when Owen Paul wasted his own time by forgetting to mime, we all just dusted our embarrassment off and carried on.

That they eventually employed Alan Titchmarsh is just a middle-aged jumper chat bonus.

Loose Women? *Cash in the Attic on tour*? Without Birmingham it would be the potter's wheel for you.

JB

No. 34: Indie Coffee Shops and their Fucking Lovely Cupcakes

Bone-idle Brummies have been loitering in coffee shops since way before the likes of Starbucks came over here with their 87,000 different drink combinations, getting our names wrong and shirking their corporation tax.

There were several coffee shops in Brum as far back as the '50s, with exotic-sounding names such as The Kardomah, El Torro, The Mexicana, The Gi-Gi, and The (um) Scorpion. The only decision to be made was 'one lump or two', and everyone's name was bab.

Genuine Bohemian and adopted Brummie, Andre Drucker, opened La Boheme coffee shop in Aston Street, which presumably kept neighbouring firefighters' caffeine levels topped up so that they were alert and ready to deal with any impending emergency. He managed to prevent Aston uni students from getting their caffeine fix by playing only classical music on the jukebox.

Drucker had a sweet tooth and was a bit miffed that he couldn't buy any decent cakes in Brum. In those days it wasn't commonplace for amateur bakers to battle it out to knock up a show-stopping Schwarzwalder-kirschtorte on your telly box.

To satisfy his sugar cravings, he opened a combination coffee shop and cake shop in fashionable Moseley (natch), but it nearly went tits-up as hipsters of yore had not yet developed their culture-vulture tenden-cies. They were more used to iced buns than pricey fancy-pants Viennese patisserie, but they were soon hooked on the new high-quality European sugar-rush. Drucker went on to open many more branches, start-ing the trend for coffee shop chains and becoming a bastard at the exact point he opened his third.

JG

No. 35: Not Admitting your Mistakes

Inventor of <u>fizzy pop</u>, Joseph Priestley made other contributions to our society too. On April 15, 1770 — not ten years before he would move to Birmingham — he recorded his discovery of Indian gum's ability to erase lead pencil marks. He wrote, "I have seen a substance excellently adapted to the purpose of wiping from paper the mark of black lead pencil." And did so in ink, which pissed him off when he discovered he'd made a cock-up.

Priestley called them 'rubbers', and they made their way into the pencil cases of schoolkids: amusing classmates of people called Jon for years to come. It also gave PR people, politicians, capitalists, and other liars a sense that it was OK simply to pretend that you'd done nothing wrong. We love that.

Viva Joey P, and viva his home town (1780-91) of Birmingham.

JB

No. 36: School

They were the best days of your life, 'they' will tell you. 'They', being everyone except Bryan Adams who is definite on the point of June, July and August of 1969 being better. What 'they' will neglect to tell you is that those days wouldn't be how they are without the city of Birmingham. Bryan however, never stops going on about Brum's own postal reformer, and world cup winner, Sir Rowland Hill.

You see at the age of twelve, before inventing <u>the post</u> and <u>the stamp</u> to go with it, Hill became a student-teacher in his father's school. In 1819 he took over the school, called Hill Top, and moved it from town to establish the Hazelwood School in Edgbaston. He called it an "educational refraction of [our man] Priestley's ideas", and it became a model for public education for the emerging middle classes. It wanted to give sufficient knowledge, skills and understanding to allow a student to continue self-education through a life "most useful to society and most happy to himself". The school building, which Hill designed, included innovations including a science laboratory, a swimming pool, and forced air heating.

In the book *Plans for the Government and Liberal Instruction of Boys in Large Numbers Drawn from Experience* (1822) he argued for kindness instead of caning, and moral influence rather than fear, for maintaining in school discipline. And some would say that's where it all went wrong, but it's certainly where the schools we know today come from.

And as Bryan Adams will no-doubt tell you, everything Sir Rowland Hill would do, he'd do it for you. And Birmingham, of course.

JB

No. 37: Vile Products of the Welfare System

Every tragedy has a beginning, and sadly one of the greatest tragedies of our time begins here, in fair Birmingham. For it was here, in the workshop of the world, that social housing was really born and with it was wrought death and ruin upon the land.

For decades, sick-leftists have praised their liberal hero Joseph Chamberlain for giving them the Lebensraum to live feckless lives, and for granting them the license they needed to beat the women they hate within the walls of homes paid for by hard-working Britons like YOU. Joe saw the slums and ramshackle utility production provided for the poor of Birmingham by private enterprise and his communist instincts kicked in. The Stalinist-before-Stalin's *Artisans' and Labourers' Dwellings Improvement Act* paved the way for huge slum clearances and the building of ~~social housing~~ dole-dwellers' mansions on our beautiful countryside. His work was the start of nearly one hundred years of pandering to those who just don't want to work hard.

Thankfully we are beginning to turn a corner, and once the precariat are rightfully stripped of shelter, murder will once again be the rightful preserve of those who do the right thing: men of good social standing, the educated, and the hard working business owners who make Britain great.

If they want a 3D TV, they'll have to pay for it out of their allotted fifty three pounds a week.   *- HW*

No. 38: That Smell of Eggs

Philosophically one can't really understand a concept until you can give it a name. You might get a head-achey feeling when walking down Oxford Road in Moseley in the autumn but until you're old enough to describe it as 'smelling like poppers' you won't really know why.

Or you might want a name for the semi-circular gap at the front of a gig, between performer and audience, that isn't filled until the venue is. Without one you won't be able to discuss the space itself. It's called a 'King's Heath' by the way, and the process of needing these names is called intentionality.

So we are again indebted to Mr Joseph Priestley for naming that weird smell of eggs that lets you know that there's a catalytic converter in the area — or that someone's guts are playing up. It's down to a lack of "vitriolic acid air" as he called it or sulphur dioxide (SO_2, to those with CSE chemistry) which should be there and faintly smelly rather than the pungent hydrogen sulphide.

Priestley, we can be sure, never denied it. But he supplied it. Hoorah for Birmingham!

JB

No. 39: The Weather

"Earlier on today, apparently, a woman rang the BBC
and said she heard there was a hurricane on the way…
well, if you're watching, don't worry, there isn't!"

Oh, Michael Fish you were a weatherman. And so
was John Kettley, and so was Bill Giles, and so was Ian
McCaskill. And with one slip of the tongue and your
magnetic cloud things, you failed to prevent Britain
being warned of a storm the like of which might nearly kill René out of *'Allo 'Allo*. (This entry really is one
for the teenagers, who with their smartphone weather
apps know that it's bloody hot right now without even
needing to look up. Magic. We used to have to take the
word of some amusingly suited men who showed their
armpits when pointing to bits of Scotland.)

In January 2007 Blues needed to re-lay their football
pitch. Thrifty as ever, they bought second hand: a
spare pitch from the new Wembley Stadium and the
club consulted John Kettley on the weather conditions
for laying it that week. Kettley predicted it would just
be the average amount of rainfall and, as you might
expect, the torrential storms washed the pitch away.

If this piece isn't taking you back into the past enough,
let's look at where 'the weather' comes from. Is it
round here, maybe? Well, yes it is.

The use of weather charts in a modern sense began
in the middle portion of the 19th century and it was
Birmingham's Sir Francis Galton who created the first
weather maps in order to devise a theory on storm

systems. These were printed in the papers, and people loved them — leading to the way we get weather information right to this day.

Brum, eh? What a scorcher.

JB

No. 40: Dangerous Dogs

Dogs, as anyone knows, are descended from wolves. However, experiments have shown that wolves are entirely undomesticated: they are sort of fine as puppies, but once they reach about 16 weeks old they become uncontrollable, extremely territorial and, before you know it, will very aggressively resist any human attempt to tell them what to do. Which sounds very much like my dogs, now that I come to think about it.

Anyway, it was these lupine personality traits that humans sought to breed out of wolves in order, initially, to put them to work, and they did this through a process of selective breeding. The most docile cub from a litter was selected and bred with a similarly docile wolf cub from another, producing an offspring from the subsequent litter that magnified the desirable traits of its parents. And so on, and on, until you get Lassie.

Apparently, in just nine generations of selective breeding, you can get from a tiny, chihuahua-sized thing to something that would give Digby, the Biggest Dog in the World a run for his money. If that indeed is the case, it seems reasonable to suggest that it would not have taken too long to remove all of the wolf-like tendencies from the pack, and so began man's unique relationship with dogs.

The vast majority of dogs are not put to work these days, as their ancestors were, and instead are very much part of the family unit. The process of taking a wild animal and turning it into something you cuddle and pamper was a smooth ride.

So, would it surprise you to know that the man who threw a spanner in the works was a Brummie? Of course it wouldn't.

James Hinks, although born in Ireland, lived most of his life in Birmingham and, when he wasn't in prison, ran The Sportsman Ale House on Worcester Street. Like Hinks, the pub is long gone and is now that bit where the buses go underneath the Bull Ring and emerge by Moor St Station. As well as a publican and occasional jailbird, Hinks was a keen dog breeder and kept kennels on-site to house his canine brood.

In 1860, Hinks decided to combine the speed and dexterity of terriers with the tenacity of the bulldog, ostensibly in order to combat the problem of vermin in the city slums. He is credited with creating a breed of dog known as the English Bull Terrier, which is the sort of dog that would give the Daily Mail a heart attack. This new, quicker, bigger, stronger and more ferocious dog eventually found a willing and regular clientele amongst the patrons of Hinks's boozer.

Pissed-up blokes buying dogs in city centre pubs. What can go possibly go wrong there?

CH

No. 41: Breakdancing

OK, so James Brown got down and Afrika Bambaataa saw b-boy and the freak as a way to change the World with his Zulu Nation. But that was back in the '70s and was that really likely ever to cross-over?

Okay, yes, so the Rock Steady Crew were busting up the East Coast (not Lowestoft) in the early '80s but were they ever more than one-hit wonders?

No, what really made sure that street dance hit the mainstream in the UK and kept it there 30 years later — battling with comic opera singers and amusing dogs on Saturday night telly — was the crew from Studio Three of ATV on Broad Street.

Tiswas introduced controlled anarchy to television, and launched the careers of swan-killer Chris Tarrant, Midland Arts Centre climbing-wall builder Bob Carolgees and Shakespearian luvvie Lenny Henry. It also launched a thousand paper plates covered in shaving foam, countless buckets of water over minor public figures, and the only pop video to include the singers walking around the Hall of Memory in Centenary Square.

It also gave us 'the dying fly'. introduced by Jasper Carrot, the Brummie stylings of lying on your back waving your arms and legs in the air was what really make breakdancing what it is today. So ingrained into British culture was 'the dying fly' that the dance at one point soared high in the RoSPA list of common causes of household injury.

Without *Tiswas*, no breakdancing. Without Birmingham, no *Tiswas*. This is what they want.

JB

No. 42: Startup Culture

When Matthew Boulton, James Watt, and William Murdoch stood at the bottom of Broad Street and stuck some post-its on the wall to plan their first sprint, little did they know they would set in motion a revolution that would see the word 'silicon' put in front of every inanimate object known to man.

For when the three luminaries banded together at their first stand-up meeting to build their minimum viable steam engine (the first two week sprint yielded nothing more than a kettle on stilts) they had unwittingly invented startup culture.

It is said that Matthew Boulton first gained the money to build the Boulton and Watt steam engine, the invention which would bring about the industrial revolution, from an initial round of seed funding together with the money he raised from selling his original company, a chain of tea bars. The tea bars themselves were the very first copy of an already successful social network, the coffee house (the chain later failed owing to debts mounted up through a large unpaid tax bill).

Every morning, before starting work, Boulton, Watt and Murdoch would gather together on a plinth at the top of Broad Street and, in turn, tell each other what they did yesterday, what they were going to do today, and what their blockers were. Their work would be packaged into short pieces of work, called 'stories' (one example, sourced from company records was: "As a mine owner, I would like to condense my steam, so I can use less coal").

The success of the trio's startup attracted the attention of other would-be West Midlands entrepreneurs, including Josiah Wedgwood, who did something with plates (records are unclear on this), and Erasmus Darwin, who despite coming from Lichfield, braved the staff shortages and delays of the cross-city line to Birmingham to meet with other like-minded individuals.

But it was another member of Birmingham's startup community that would threaten to tear the community apart — Joseph Priestley began writing a series of scurrilous pamphlets about the burgeoning scene, but after refusing to pay contributors, he was driven out of the city by pitchfork-wielding journalists. While in exile, he wrote further pamphlets attacking the people who drove him out, as well as making a healthy living espousing controversial opinions at public events for money.

Although the steam engine was a success, the 'fail fast' culture yielded many failures, including a new monetary system based on calculations made by teams of children using abacuses, and a driverless horse and cart, which lost control on its maiden voyage down Bull Street, killing dozens.

While there were failures and controversies, Birmingham's startup scene grew and grew, until there were none. Over time, the city's startups grew into bigger businesses, until they looked from small to big, and big to small, and it was impossible to say which was which.

SH

No. 43: Environmental Catastrophe

Technically, you could argue that, as the cradle of the Industrial Revolution, Birmingham and the Midlands will eventually gift to all humankind a catastrophic environmental collapse that will ultimately destroy the human race. Some might say it'll be our just desserts for pillaging the planet's resources. But knowing what form our destruction will take? Well that can be laid at our door too.

The time was 11:15pm, the place, latitude 35, some 24 degrees west of Greenwich, the ship, the Guinevere. Our narrator and his new bride watch as mysterious red glowing lights fall from the sky into the ocean. As the story unfolds, it becomes clear that an alien life-force has colonised the ocean depths. In theory, we could have lived peacefully together, co-existing in our separate corners of the Earth. But no, the humans have to go and fuck it up it, sending down submarines to investigate and, when these are destroyed, dropping nukes into the sea to upset the new arrivals. What follows is an escalation of attack and counter-attack until the aliens unleash their most devastating blow: they melt the polar ice caps. This causes sea levels to rise, flooding many major cities and resulting in social and political meltdown across the globe. Serves us bloody right.

So goes *The Kraken Wakes*, the 1953 novel by Dorridge-born and Edgbaston-raised father of modern science fiction, John Wyndham. John loved nothing better than to dream up new and exciting ways to destroy humanity, be it malevolent gladioli (*The Day of the Triffids*); weird blonde kids (*The Midwich Cuckoos*); nazi clones (*The Plan for Chaos*), or <u>nuclear holocaust</u> — twice (*The Outward Urge* and *The Chrysalids*).

Must've been a fun guy to go down the pub with.

SF

No. 44: Musical Differences

All bands eventually get back together, except for the only two that you might actually want to see again: Slade and The Smiths. They all get back together because they all split up and then find they need the money, and the reason they split up is called 'musical differences'. The 'differences' being 'the difference between the cash they each pocket in royalties' and the 'musical' being *Oliver!* on VHS on the tour bus.

Oasis ran out of ideas, yes, but the creative bankruptcy just made it all the more galling for Liam that it his brother was earning in the region of seven times what he was: because Noel wrote the big hit songs.

Readers of Morrissey's autobiography (and hi readers, these spaces in between groups of sentences are paragraphs) will know that El Moz and Johnny Marr got 40 per cent each while the other two Smiths got 10. And they'll know all about the recriminations afterwards. And what the judge in the court case had for breakfast. When these bands split, like so much from Up North, it's bitter rather than mild.

But they wouldn't have split if it wasn't for Birmingham.

Because back in 1914 as the world geared up for War, Birmingham invented musical differences: there just wasn't enough real conflict around.

The *Daily Mirror* was first with the news about the music hall smash hit *It's a long long way to Tipperary* and gives us a story with all the classic hallmarks of musical differences. Drink, millions killed on the Somme, and a fish stall outside a pub in the Black Country. It's so Led Zeppelin it hurts.

The song was written by Harry Williams, from Erdington, and first sung with his musical partner Jack Judge, from Oldbury. Harry did the music, Jack was really just a frontman: all hips, lips and clogs.

They called the song *It's A Long Way to Connemara* and Jack regularly performed it in concert. Three years later, Judge took a five-shilling bet to compose and perform a song in a day at the New Market Inn in Stalybridge.

Jack changed Connemara to Tipperary, winning the bet and delighting his audience with the catchy 'new' song. The rest is payola history, even Wikipedia keeps dismissing Birmingham's role in "the song that won the war". He even carried on gigging the same material long after the partnership dried up, so maybe Birmingham can also claim to have invented Beady Eye.

And then Manchester built a fucking statue: in Stalybridge. Which is in Manchester when it suits them, much like Salford.

One word? How would famous Mancunian™ Karl Marx have liked it if Engels altered the first line of The Communist Manifesto to "A ghost is haunting Europe" and claimed he wrote it after a night on the sauce at the Flapper because he had made a bet with Pierre-Joseph Proudhon?

So Manchester stole our song, but by being in a huff about it we laid the road map for a thousand disputes about the means of songwriting production. If those bands had stuck to the words of Marx and Engels and, like those guys, split everything down the middle they'd have been okay but The Smiths, New Order, Oasis and even the Stone Roses took their cue from Birmingham.

Is Birmingham responsible for, *Das Kapital*? Nah, but it is Das Second City.

JB & JH

No. 45: Car Horns

Human beings are strange animals. One of our oddest traits is the belief that certain objects are made not of earthly or man-made materials, such as iron, carbon, cotton, or paper, but of fucking magic.

Some items are thought to bring us good luck, such as horseshoes, or rabbits' feet, or particular types of coin, whilst other things, such as wood (when touched), or salt (when thrown over the shoulder), are thought to ward off bad luck. Not only that, but combinations of apparently unrelated items are either thought to bring about very, very bad luck (new shoes on the table, walking under ladders), or signs of impending very, very good luck (bird shit on the shoulder, black cats crossing your path).

Then, of course, there are the other items, such as a fridges, that are seen simply as white boxes that keep stuff cold and are not thought to contain any magic properties at all. Although, in the case of fridges, the question of whether or not the light goes off when you close the door remains a mystery.

It's all very odd and arbitrary. But in Birmingham, as you'd expect, things are every-so-slightly different.

Whilst we Brummies might hold with some of those strange superstitions and beliefs, what sets us apart is that we have long been in the business of creating, with our enquiring minds and ingenious hands, what others around the world perceive to be magic.

Take, for example, the Brummie engineer, Oliver Lucas: In 1910, he invented the car horn, and that is the perfect example. Here are some things it can do:

• A quick and cheerful double-toot of the horn at 5am can alert your mate that you have arrived to pick him up, but it won't wake up every single dog and baby along the same street.

• If a section of the working population is engaged in industrial action, you can directly support their strike by honking your horn as you drive past them on your way to your own place of work.

• It can tell a person walking down the street in a totally non-creepy way that you, as luck would have it, are indeed free this Friday night and that, yes, you would love to take them out in order to get to know them better.

• Despite only emitting a harsh, single tone, your horn is nevertheless capable of playing along in tune with the record currently playing on the car radio. Owners of multi-tonal, novelty horn sounds believe other people think they are cool, which amounts to the same thing.

Perhaps most magically of all: the car horn is capable of clearing that traffic jam in front of your vehicle and the magic properties of the horn grow exponentially if everyone in the same jam joins in.

In fairness to Lucas, of course, none of this rampant bellendery is his fault. He originally invented the horn as a safety measure, having foreseen the inherent danger of giving idiot humans access to powerful and heavy moving metal things. Indeed, more than just a whiff of Lucas's original intention can still be seen enshrined in The Highway Code, Rule 92, which pertains to use of the horn:

Use only while your vehicle is moving and you need to warn other road users of your presence. Never sound your horn aggressively. You MUST NOT use your horn while stationary on the road [or] when driving in a built up area between the hours of 11.30 pm and 7.00 am, except when another vehicle poses a danger.

Brummies, as has been discussed elsewhere in this book, have a somewhat unique approach to road use, and I'm just as bad, so I'd like it to be noted before I continue that I'm not lobbing stones from my greenhouse here. However, I'm sure that we can all agree that the paragraph above would probably account for less than 1% of global car horn use, and that the other 99% is just people being dicks.

So, just like nuclear missiles, heavy metal, and tennis, the car horn is yet another Brummie invention that grew dangerous teeth once the rest of the world took it to their hearts. Yet again, we are left feeling like Charlton Heston at the end of *Planet of the Apes*, weeping as we see a beautiful creation destroyed by the madness of other men.

It's worth pointing out that Lucas was simply building on an existing Brummie tradition of inventing things that politely told people to get the fuck out of your way when you were operating transport machinery at speed. It was here, in 1877, that John Richard Dedicoat, an apprentice of James Watt invented the direct predecessor to the car horn: the bicycle bell. And look at how annoying some people have become once armed with that.

Dedicoat, incidentally, also invented the pencil sharpener, a contraption that was useful to many, but in particular to the traffic policeman and parking wardens whose functions came into being primarily to curb the selfish transgressions of vehicular knobends the world over. In other words, Dedicoat helped to solve the problem he inspired his fellow Brummie to inadvertently contribute to the creation of.

And that, right there, is further evidence of our collective, creative genius and time-hopping, 360 degree thinking that proves we Brummies do indeed think of everything.

CH

No. 46: Star Wars

In the 1970s a young filmmaker named George Lucas began putting together an ambitious project to bring us the story of a boy, a girl and a universe.

He took a pretty standard Proppian fairy tale structure, added some Flash Gordon adventure serialisation tropes, and stopped by Kurosawa for some eastern mysticism and warrior codes. And no one knew what the hell he was talking about. Desperate to show people his vision he assembled a rough cut of the film. The problem: he needed to show the complicated space battles he'd planned for the finale.

Some 35 years earlier Birmingham's shadow factories had been churning out Lancaster bombers, Spitfires and all kind of airborne weaponry, to win the Battle of Britain and generally show Jerry a thing or two.

A few years later the stories of those magnificent flying machines became WWII movies, full of daring-do and high-altitude dogfights. Lucas literally took those movies and cut the battles into his space opera as place holders, showing how things would go down. The rough cut did enough to convince the money men in Hollywood that the *Star Wars* was going to be worth persevering with. With his project saved, Lucas reproduced those dogfights shot-for-shot, using his own plastic models and a black sheet for space where Northern Europe used to be. And so it goes, Birmingham's factories put the bearded Jedi master on the road to building his own Galactic Empire.

No Brum, no X-Wings, simple as that, but we ain't going to apologise for Jar Jar Binks — for that you only have yourselves to blame.

JH

No. 47: Local Radio

It comes into its own in a crisis, you know. It's how
people know that roads are slippery or schools closed
because it snowed, other than that the ground is
covered in snow. And despite attempts by both 'market
forces' and 'stupid government pandering BBC Director Generals obsessed with nothing more than their
jobs and the bottom line' it's still going.

It's the place for the gentle discussion, followed by
great tunes from M People. Or on commercial local
radio: an advert for a local loan shark, followed by M
People and the Lighthouse Family, broadcast from an
industrial estate in Greater London. But what would
we do without it, eh?

And, of course, what would we do without Birmingham? "Witton calling" were the first words on Radio
5IT, a station based on Electric Avenue, Witton in
1922 and it was the first BBC radio broadcast outside
London. A commitment that the national broadcaster hasn't really kept up. Local radio: another export
we've given to prop up Manchester.

JB

No. 48: TV Box Sets

The TV box set is a thing. It's so much a thing that it has now detached itself from its own material: a box set is no longer a TV series collected as a set and presented in a box, it is now simply the thing, collected, and placed in a set completely agnostic to the process of boxing. Here's an example: Sky TV actively promotes watching 'box sets' as part of its online services. So you can watch a box set on a computer without ever seeing a box, because the box doesn't exist except as a metaphor within the marketing material. When I challenged them as to how a video on the Internet could be described as being in a box, Sky's social media people seemed confused by the question as though — through some Orwellian process — a box set had always *never* been in a box.

But why should a company like Sky be so keen to sell us a TV box set in the first place? Well, Sky is a very shrewd and successful media company, so their people know about things like supply and demand. They also know about trend-spotting and how to make the most of changes in viewing practices. They've spotted that you like box sets of glossy telly — they probably knew before you did — and so they want to sell them to you.

TV box sets have been around for a long time, as anyone who has ever been to Oxfam will tell you. (Next time you're in there, go and find the VHS set of an early season of *Friends* that they will definitely have in). But they didn't really become a *thing* until the turn of the century.

Over the past ten or fifteen years the box set has become an important part of our TV viewing and purchasing practices. The box set has spawned long running broadsheet columns which both chronicle and feed our love of the box set as a format (the *Guardian's* 'your next box set' being a prime example). If we looked into it I bet we'd find that box set sales have helped prop up HMV as it lurches drunkenly towards high street oblivion, especially at Christmastime, because we all know that things become intrinsically more gift-like when they are placed in a prepackaged box. (How else to explain the fact that last Christmas I bought a mere one pint of supermarket lager for my brother in law for £10 — a premium of around 350% — because it happened to be in a tin?). Box set viewing seems to be a cultural practice that touches all parts of society. On the one hand, my Mum has a penchant for nostalgic reissue box sets of TV shows from the 1980s, while on the other, Sarah Ferguson and her kids apparently spend whole weekends under a duvet watching them. (Well, let's face it, they've not got much else to do unless a *King Ralph* level catastrophe happens).

At the heart of much of the cult of the box set is the concept of 'the marathon': the practice of gorging oneself on telly, as enabled by the presence of a great deal of it. In a box. And I think it's fair to say that we wouldn't have the box set marathon, nor indeed the strangely remediated idea of a box set that is not in a box, if it wasn't for England's second city. For you see it was in North Birmingham that the first seeds of the box set as a phenomenon were sown for it was there that the actor Martin Shaw grew up and first learnt his craft.

In his early career he lent a hand with a little television series called something like *The Coronation Street* — some sort of provincial northern morality play, I think? — before putting in some solid work as the face of the Ford Capri. Other work in television and the theatre followed. Then in 1977, the dashing young brummie was cast as Doyle, of Bodie and Doyle fame, in the action series *The Professionals*, the series to which we must now draw our attention.

The Professionals was the story of right-wing super cops who work outside the rules to stop nuclear bombs. If that sounds familiar, it's because in Shaw's performance we see the template for Jack Bauer, and in the show we see many of the hallmarks of Jack's own show, *24*. Bodie, Doyle, Bauer: poster boys for robust methods, for being uncompromising, tough and doing the unthinkable. And if they can be tough and do the unthinkable to someone who is brown, well all the better.

It was *24* that heralded the new dawn of the box set (it even earned a name check from Her Royal Fergs as her favourite one) by taking the fascist police state fantasies of *The Professionals* and wedding them to a powerful hook: real-time. *24* provides a one season long story arc, delivered as one hour of television per one hour of narrative. *The Professionals* was a serial, giving complete narratives in each episode, but *24* offered us weekly riddles, not weekly solutions, which were cleverly tied to the beat of a clock that was always counting, pushing us on, on, on. As an audience we wanted to watch more, more, more, more and so *24* in box set form was hard to resist.

The case then is made, and it's a simple one: no Birmingham, no Martin Shaw, and no *Professionals*, no CI5, no CTU, no Jack Bauer and no *24*, no *24* no TV box set marathons.

No Birmingham? I really don't know what Sarah Ferguson would do with her time.

JH

No. 49: Conference Centres

Anyone who regularly travels by train between Birmingham and Coventry will know that the National Exhibition Centre (NEC) is a little like Enid Blyton's *Magic Faraway Tree*. As the train pulls into Birmingham International station, every train regular is wondering, which land is at the NEC this week? If the carriage is suddenly full of perfume, giggling women and designer handbags, it's probably the Clothes Show. If it's wall-to-wall North Face, it'll be a hiking event or a Christian rock concert and if there's a faint pong of wet dog, you know that it's the Liberal Democrat conference.

The NEC is the UK's largest conference centre and it is fitting that it is in Birmingham, home to the world's first ever purpose-built permanent exhibition hall. Bingley Hall opened on Broad Street in 1850. Designed by local architect J. A. Chatwin, who also worked on the Houses of Parliament, Bingley Hall must have wowed the Victorian public. Its interior space stretched over an acre and a quarter and held 25,000 people in five rooms. It had ten entrance doors and had used nearly 12,000 feet of 21-inch glass in its construction. Of course, just a year later Birmingham-wannabe London launched the Great Exhibition and the rather showy Crystal Palace left Bingley Hall looking small in comparison. But, the Birmingham venue outlived its metropolitan rival by five decades, before also finally succumbing to a fire in 1984.

For more than a century, Bingley Hall hosted shows on dogs, cows, cars and boats, fireplaces, chrysanthemums and poultry. It was the place to go for boxing matches, cycling competitions, circuses, concerts, cinema and religious and political rallies. Modern politicians reading bad jokes to empty conference halls would be devastated to hear that in 1888 Gladstone made a speech at Bingley Hall that attracted over 30,000 people. Glass had to be removed from the ceiling to make space to squeeze more people in and so many fainted and had to be lifted out that a kind of reverse-crowd-surfing occurred. Although, as his oratory was over two hours long, you can't blame the audience for trying to escape. It became the first political speech ever to be recorded, as Thomas Edison's phonograph had been shipped from the US to the event too. So, it could be argued that without Birmingham we might also have no *Question Time* or *Any Questions* — perhaps not even one Dimbleby-fronted programme. In fact, perhaps the fainting people being lifted out of the Hall were thinking, "It's being recorded, so I'll catch up later before Andrew Neil comes on and starts talking about Blue Nun".

Later in its history, mid-twentieth-century lofts and broom cupboards bore witness to Bingley Hall's annual visit from the Ideal Home Exhibition. Gadgets would be bought that promised to revolutionise domestic life, were used once and then abandoned in dust-gathering ignominy. Making Bingley Hall a bit like a Betterware catalogue (who are based in Castle Vale, tat fans), only including a day out along with the inevitable cycle of enticement, confusion and disappointment.

If you've read the foreword to this book, you'll already know that Stewart Lee saw the Wombles play a show at Bingley Hall but, as well as giant recycling-obsessed rodents, Bingley Hall also rocked out to bands like the Yardbirds, Deep Purple, ZZ Top, the Animals and Hawkwind. Motorhead once had to abandon their encore at the venue when Lemmy was too, ahem, 'tired' to go back on. Recently, Queen legend and badger-protector Brian May has revealed that he was inspired to write *We Will Rock You* after playing a gig at Bingley Hall, and also presumably where Freddie liked to buy his <u>vacuums</u>.

The story of the world's first exhibition hall came to an abrupt end in early 1984 when it was destroyed in a fire at the Midland Caravan, Camping and Leisure Exhibition. We can only speculate as to whether this was caused by inattentive use of a Calor gas stove or a faulty barbeque ignition kit, but it is understood that the incident led Brian May to write the Queen hit *Flash*.

Rising phoenix-like from the flames, on the hallowed ground of Bingley Hall, came the International Conference Centre. This is the zenith of late twenti-eth-century conferencing. It's hosted the G8, Nato and the first meeting of the UK Cabinet held outside London in 90 years. Not to mention a few party political conferences that notably failed to have them fainting in the aisles.

Yes, the ICC can feel corporate. Yes, lanyards and lattes are never far from one's line of vision. But the spirit of the old Bingley Hall is still here. The ghosts of circus performers, carpet baggers and horse breeders still haunt this turf — and that of every conference venue that followed. If you're at the World of Pencil Sharpeners on a wet Wednesday in February, be proud of those who have taken the path before you. Channel Lemmy when you're offered a business card; tell them that the only card you need is, "The Ace Of Spades".

LHB

No. 50: Exchange Students

When we were at school a mate of mine would occasionally turn up at things during the summer with a weird sidekick: a French kid called Xavier. Xavier was an exchange student, sent over for weeks at a time to learn English how it is *really spoken*. Unfortunately for M. et Mme. Frenchie, they'd sent Xavier to hang out with a load of teenage boys so all Xavier learnt was how to say "I ave gaz" and then belch very loudly.

But Xavier wouldn't have got that far if it wasn't for Birmingham for we had our very own exchange student, America's Benjamin Franklin, who used to come over to brush up on science and invention as it *really happens* by spending weeks in the 18th century working alongside the gentlemen of the Lunar Society who, it turned out, actually did have <u>gas</u>.

JH

No. 51: Eugenics

I'm not a psychoanalyst, but in the case of Francis
Galton I'll have a look. Grandson of Erasmus Darwin (erstwhile Lunar Society member, poet, naturalist,
and inventor of the PA system), and hence cousin
of Charles who was 13 years his senior, he devoted
most of his life to promoting the idea that genius was
hereditary.

His other grandfather was Samuel 'John' Galton, from
Duddeston and also a Lunar Society member, who
was a prominent Quaker and arms manufacturer who
seems to have excelled in many things. Except 'getting
interesting nicknames' and the pacifist bit of Quaker-
ism.

Francis's dad, known as Samuel Tertius Galton, wrote
papers on economics and his older brother Darwin
Galton became High Sheriff of Warwickshire. Can
you feel the familial pressure to succeed yet?

He was supposedly something of a child prodigy,
reading local hero Shakespeare's work at the age of six,
attending King Edward's School, and studying medicine at Birmingham General Hospital. Then he took
a maths degree at Trinity College Cambridge: where
the cracks began to show. A nervous breakdown and
the death of his father led him to chuck it all up, rebel
and become an explorer. With the Royal Geographical
Society.

He turned out to be rather good at it, with pioneering
cartographic studies of what would become Namib-

ia, and the best-selling book *The Art of Travel* which offered "practical advice for the Victorian on the move". His map-making skills also contributed to him developing the first <u>weather maps</u>. He was a credit to his family.

But they fuck you up, your grandfathers and their Lunar Society mates, they might not mean to, but they do. And so do your cousins.

Galton became rather obsessed with the work of Charles Darwin, and *The Origin of Species* became the jumping-off point for what we would consider now a rather darker area of study. Taking the chapter on the breeding of domestic animals to a slightly illogical conclusion, he developed and gave the name to an area of science that we might term '*un*natural selection': eugenics.

Developing all sorts of analytic and statistical prcesses on the way, he looked for evidence that human ability was heredity. In his book *Hereditary Genius* he detailed how the number of 'eminent' relatives dropped off as you moved from first degree to second to third. He took this to be evidence of inheritance of abilities; his theory being: it's not what you know, or even who you know, but who your dad knew. Biblically.

Rather rejecting the idea that hanging out with lots of other smart people in a safe environment, with money and a shitload of guns to back you up if needed, might just help a tiny bit in nurturing 'eminence', Francis went all out down the genetic route. He suggested encouraging selective breeding in humans to improve the stock, a policy beloved of all sorts of right-wing nutjobs ever since. He also believed that a system of 'marks' should be developed to identify 'families of merit'. There is no record of whether these would be best as a sort of six pointed yellow star.

Galton, of course, would claim that the ideas were good for the whole human race. And, in a passage in his book that could be headed "I'm not racist, but…", he suggested that "the pride of race" should be encouraged but "the better sort of emigrants and refugees from other lands [should be] invited and welcomed, and their descendants naturalised." And we might believe him too, had he not written a letter to *The Times* espousing the idea of giving Africa to the Chinese instead of the 'inferior' people who lived there already.

And if you want any more evidence that he was a — very smart and well-connected — wrong-un, Galton also invented the questionnaire and therefore market research.

Francis Galton then, a little from column A, a little from column B, and a little from the column marked 'oh my God, he didn't just say that did he?'.

JB

No. 52: Shit Shoes

If you've seen any coverage of a recent Oscar ceremony, or any Oscar ceremony, you'll know it's all about the clothes. The women's clothes. The women's bodies, the ladies' bras. Male attendees get to dig out evening dress and pass without comment. It's an everyday sexist world, but let's turn the male gaze on its head. Or feet rather.

Posh men's shoes are always shiny, and that's hard to keep up. Unless you have a basic military training, polishing leather is boring, hard, and messy. Luckily for the servants of the rich and famous, there is an alternative. And for that alternative the maids in Manhattan have to thank: Birmingham.

Back in 1793 a chap called Hand, in Birmingham of course, obtained a patent for preparing flexible leather with a glaze and polish that renders it impervious to water and need only be wiped with a sponge to restore it to its original lustre. This is patent leather, and it's been responsible for awful shiny shoes all the way from Bacons to Freeman Hardy and Willis, to <u>Hollywood</u> (which we invented too) stars Martin Freeman, Oliver Hardy and Bruce Willis.

Birmingham: it scrubs up well. Or wipes up with a sponge easily. Or something.

JB

No. 53: Suburbia

Suburbia eh? Leafy streets, Terry and June, mock tudor, bay windows — surely that all started in Surrey or Middlesex, and spread to the rest of the country? Well no, it all started in Birmingham. Of course.

When George Cadbury moved his factory from central Birmingham to what was then rural Worcestershire he decided to create a model village. It was not just to house his workers, contrary to received wisdom, it was more ambitious than that. Open to all, it was designed as a model for how the lives of workers would be improved. The most important thing, reading his comments at the time, was to get them away from pubs and give them gardens — which proved a boon to both the local B&Q and the off-licence trade in Stirchley.

In a way though, Birmingham had already got there, with Edgbaston's Calthorpe Estate, which was one of the first planned suburbs, and a remarkably green and spacious one. It was also home to Cadbury, and he appeared to be completely enamoured with it: but more importantly, he wanted to create one for the ordinary Brummies he met in his voluntary work as a committed Quaker.

At around the same time the Garden City Association, which had fairly similar objectives, was in the ascendant. It had its first conference at Bournville, and the whole place was taken as a model for the larger, later schemes at Letchworth and Welwyn.

The whole mock medieval aesthetic of Bournville was no geographic accident. Birmingham was a centre of the Arts and Crafts movement, indeed its founder William Morris was the first President of the municipal art school (the country's first), no doubt due to being best mates with local boy Edward Burne-Jones.

Anyway, Bournville's aesthetic was basically cloned and honed for the garden cities and the later, larger garden suburb at Hampstead. They didn't seem to keep the purple signage or the pervasive smell of bitter chocolate.

Twenty years later, during the 1930s building boom, the mass builders produced a bastardised version of the whole thing and covered vast swathes of the country in the bay-windowed semis we now think of as typical suburbia. Appropriately, Birmingham then saw the biggest boom in suburb-building outside the South East.

So, next time you're passing through Hall Green, listening to the Pet Shop Boys, blame it all on George Cadbury.

JN

No. 54: The Vacuum Cleaner

Freddie Mercury liked using one while in drag, and
they make an awful mess when you empty the bag.
Apocryphally they end up in casualty departments all
around the country attached to blokes' private areas
and make a lovely rattling sound when they suck up a
coin.

The vacuum, it sucks but we can't live without it.

The manually powered domestic vacuum cleaner was
invented in 1905 by Walter Griffiths of 72 Conybere
Street, Highgate, Birmingham. It was originally patented as *Griffiths' Improved Vacuum Apparatus for Removing
Dust from Carpets*. A better name than Dirt Devil, I'm
sure you'll agree.

So Birmingham gave the world the first proper vacuum, and yet again transformed our lives: and, for the
worse, those of our dogs.

Although an electric cleaner was patented before
in 1901 by H. Cecil Booth, Griffiths' design is more
similar to modern portable cleaners. Mr Dyson will
no-doubt soon improve on it more — before moving
the manufacture to India and then making pronounce-
ments on the British economy and the lack of jobs —
but it was invented in Brum, and we're having it.

JB

No. 55: The Orwellian Nightmares of the Daily Mail

Eric Arthur Blair's *1984* provides such a compelling vision of life in a totalitarian state that it has become the founding text on which fears of undemocratic control are built. Its ideas are strong and can be easily adapted to suit almost any political purpose.

The left will shuffle in their donkey jackets and point to the opprobrium hurled at immigrants or the poor, look hard, over a plate of custard creams, and cry 'two minutes hate' at the right wing press. Libertarians call almost any attempt to do anything 'Big Brother'. But it's the likes of the Daily Mail that have taken the contents of the book most to heart.

'Orwellian' is a phrase that the Daily Mail use a lot, there are over 30 pages of search results on their website. Its use is often combined with the word 'nightmare' and almost always followed by a story about how a local council or the BBC has 'banned' the the use of a word. Or talking about black people. Or in one 'news story' I came across: broccoli.

For those that have actually read more Orwell than just *1984*, it can take a while to realise what they mean by 'Orwellian'. It turns out they don't mean going hop picking in Kent, feeling rather awkward about shooting an elephant, or being a struggling parson's daughter: it's purely about the supposed control of thought by use of language. Something the paper behind 'Hurrah for the Blackshirts' should know a lot about.

"Who controls the past controls the future; who controls the present controls the past." is the manifesto of IngSoc, the rulers of the present in *1984*. But it's all fiction, can you really think of an organisation who would write revisionist history with an agenda?

Orwell wrote *1984* as a warning not against communism, but against totalitarianism, and his visions of how propaganda becomes dangerous and becomes 'the truth' were informed by his experiences fighting for the POUM militia in the Spanish Civil War. The Spanish Republican and the English left wing presses were fed lines by the Communist Parties of Spain and Russia against their comrades in forces that differed ideologically, even when they were on the same side. Stalin's backing for the Spanish government wasn't as altruistic as it could have been. Orwell returned from the war bloodied and disillusioned, and never again trusted 'the party'.

The schisms in the left were necessary to control the ideas rather than the country, and that was seen to be more important: because realistically there was no way the Republicans could win the war. Spain's defeat and Orwell's loss of hope stemmed from that realisation: and that all came from the lack of support shown to the government of Spain by the English and French.

Foreshadowing the appeasement of Hitler in the following years, the two powers just didn't want to get involved and the refusal to sell arms to the democratically elected government of Spain meant that the Republic was doomed. The fascists had support from Germany and, crucially, Mussolini's Italy who trans-

ported General Franco and his troops back to main-
land Spain.

Orwell's ideas and book came directly from that
non-intervention and that non-intervention came directly from Birmingham. King's Heath's own Neville
Chamberlain, then Prime Minister, fought hard for the
right to stand idle and let evil triumph, even heavily
leaning on the French so they would do likewise.

He eventually got a lovely note of thanks from the
victorious Franco, a piece of paper in his hand that he
kept rather more quiet about than some.

¡No Pasaran! As they don't say at Highbury Hall.

JB

No. 56: Doctor Who

Way back in 1963, a children's educational TV programme aired and not that many people noticed — they were too upset that Aldous Huxley had died (especially Sheryl Crow). It starred an old chap who pottered around the universe in four dimensions. But without a nemesis the story was going nowhere, he wasn't much of a hero — what he needed was an evil race to battle — one that was flawless, except for the flaw that they needed a level floor.

But how would they perambulate across those even surfaces? They needed some sort of castor that kept the two bearing surfaces of an axle, fixed and moving, apart.

Luckily in 1876, in Birmingham, William Bown patented a design for the wheels of roller skates which did just this…

Then, in 1955, a young man called McFly from Hill Valley in the United States took those wheels, invented the skateboard, rock and roll and popular science fiction in a couple of days. Not less than eight years later, way back in 1963, a children's educational TV programmed aired and not that many people noticed — they were too upset that Aldous Huxley had died (especially Sheryl Crow). It starred an old chap who pottered around the universe in four dimensions. Without a nemesis the story was going nowhere, he wasn't much of a hero — what he needed was an evil race to battle — one that was flawless, except the flaw that they needed a level floor.

But how would they perambulate across those even surfaces? They needed some sort of castor that kept the two bearing surfaces of an axle, fixed and moving, apart.

Luckily in 1876, in Birmingham William Bown patented a design for the wheels of roller skates which did just this…

JB

No. 57: Responsible Capitalism

Ed Miliband probably has the toughest job in politics right now, in 2014. On paper he's up against a Tory party that doesn't hold a majority and a Liberal Democrat party that's surely going to slope off into electoral oblivion. His party and the wider liberal left are making strong cases against some of the most aggressive and damaging policies of the Tory-led government. He should be a dead cert, but he's not. Why? Simply the system is stacked against him because the battle lines have been drawn around neoliberal agendas and he has been framed as a socialist. In the Overton Window of media-friendly political debate this has left him looking a little like he's hiding behind the curtains.

In his response to that, Ed has tried to make his left-wing ideas more attractive. To do this he has moved further right on some issues while also constructing new arguments that draw on language used by those on the right.

'Responsible capitalism' is a Milibandian idea that finds an accommodation between doing business and looking out for people. This has then been interpreted as Ed meekly asking: can we make money but just do it in a nice way? I think the idea is sharper than that, about using the levers of regulation to direct the market in more humane ways. And I can tell you this: he got the idea from Birmingham.

Back in the days of the English Civil War, John Porter was the best sword maker in the land and he sold his wares here in Birmingham. Or rather he sold his wares to anyone but the King. You see Charlie's army were short on weapons for their campaign against the Parliamentarians so his people went up to Birmingham to get some of Porter's finest gear (it seems we invented being a retail destination at around this time). Porter is said to have refused to sell any arms to "that man of blood" regardless of how much money he was offered. That, of course, is not how it's supposed to work in a free market and so the confused Royalists were set upon Brum in a rage by their angry King.

The resultant Battle of Camp Hill was, by many accounts, one of the darker chapters of the war, and one in which the trained Royalist soldiers were given a run for their money by untrained, unarmed Brummies (who may or may not have been heard shouting "leave him Gary, he's not worth it mate" or "kick 'is fookin 'ed in Steve").

If that's responsible capitalism then you have my sword, Ed.

JH

No. 58: One-way Streets

Jonathan Meades likes Birmingham. Even for a public intellectual he's a contrary bugger. He spends the first chapter of his recent autobiography bemoaning the fact he wasn't a good looking enough child to attract the attentions of any pedophiles.

In his 1998 BBC programme *Heart By-Pass: Jonathan Meades Motors Through Birmingham* he fixates on Birmingham as the home of the car, the place where the first integrated garages were built. And, he says, "the first city to authorise one-way streets".

And that's our evidence, which seems rather flimsy. Except that delving into the history of the one-way street reveals just how bad everyone else seems to have been at it. An attempt was made in 1617 to introduce one-way streets near the Thames in London, where people were no doubt told which direction to Lambeth Walk in, with their thumbs in their jacket collars. It didn't work — and they didn't try again until 1800. A visitor to Barcelona can see remnants of 'donkey one way systems' in the alleys around La Ramblas, with which the town planner made an ass of himself when no one took a blind bit of notice.

Jonathan Meades's key word here is 'authorise' — this is a council job and back in the mists of time Birmingham had a rather efficient and forward-looking administration. It was responsible for sorting out housing, water and gas — all sorts of things that Birmingham enjoyed right up until the 1980s when Thatcher sold them off and kept the money. These days the council is well meaning but not so efficient. I asked the press office to tell me more about our innovation with these one-way streets: the answer that came back pointed only one way too, "We don't know. Have you tried Carl Chinn?"

JB

No. 59: Comic Sans

Font family and hatred magnet, Comic Sans MS was created by Microsoft's Vincent Connare to be the textual voice of a cartoon dog called Bob, who would in some way help people use computers. It looks friendly and soon became the Australian Question Intonation of typefaces: that is, used when the message is passive aggressive — or just plain irritating — in an effort to soften the blow.

Ignorant desktop publishers combined it with clip art to promote their bake sales and sell their unwanted furniture on workplace noticeboards across the world — and wound up hipsters something rotten in the process. Which, for a typeface, is something to be proud of.

But it, and easily-set legible fontage in general, would never have been possible without Birmingham's John Baskerville. The designer, free-thinker and atheist produced the first usable typeface in 1757 (*this one*, Baskerville) and started a publishing revolution: with an edition of Roman poetry.

Our book isn't quite Virgil, but we're honour bound to tell you that the soundtrack to *Thunderbirds* was made in Birmingham too.

JB

No. 60: Panhandling

If you don't ask, you don't get. Despite the protests of anyone who's ever wanted to make it from one end of New Street to the other, asking people for money is profitable and it will continue. Birmingham has some world class panhandling: the girl with the odd voice and dreads who needs 65p to get home to Bearwood, the squaddie who's missed his train back to base, Vernon the Big Issue seller who made a Christmas single, and not to forget the historical local begging on a global stage that bought us the ICC with all that European money

So would you be surprised to see that the city invented a certain type of begging? Of course not, but it happened some way before there was a city to beg in.

In the Domesday Book, Birmingham is recorded as one homestead: worth about two goats. But in 1166 the Lord of the Manor Peter de Birmingham obtained a royal charter from Henry II permitting him to hold a weekly market "at his castle at Birmingham" and crucially to charge tolls on the market's traffic. Money, in effect, for just passing up New St.

This one of the earliest of these charters that would be granted in England, and definitely the cheekiest: imagine charging people to come into a rough area to look at some stalls of turnips and mead. Not only did Lord de Birmingham invent panhandling, it seems like he started the first farmers' market. Come to Birmingham, it's yer money we're after, baby.   - *JB*

No. 61: Infographics

When we were a city of a thousand trades, we had men to produce thousands of words to tell the story. One such was Joseph Priestley who essentially didn't ever shut up, producing hundreds of pamphlets and books on philosophy, science, religion and even <u>grammar</u>. But that age of reason is long gone: our civic leaders now find it difficult to work out that people are unlikely to pony up for having their grass cuttings taken away.

Numbers and facts are hard, so it's lucky that the power of a thousand words can now be delivered so easily by: pictures of toilet signs at different sizes, circles overlapping, and maps — all laid out like a pastel-coloured '30s variety bill poster.

In short, thank heaven for the infographic. Or, thank Birmingham rather.

For you see, Joseph Priestley was not just a polymath but completely lithographically incontinent — and in 1769 he published *A New Chart of History* in which:

"the horizontal line conveys an idea of the duration of fame, influence, power and domination. A vertical reading conveys an impression of the contemporaneity of ideas, events and people. The number or density of entries... tells us about the vitality of any age."

An that's a clear as it can be. Birmingham invented the infographic, saving the future communicators the bother of having to work out coherent sentences to put on the Internet. If only Birmingham had invented the Venn diagram too… or perhaps it did. Keep 'em peeled.

JB

No. 62: Israel, and the Middle East Problem

Of all the great things Birmingham has given the world — there's more than 101, look out for the sequel — nothing quite provides a glow of pride like the bloodshed in the Middle East.

At the close of the 19th century, an area known as Palestine was home to Arabs, Muslims, Christians and Jews, who lived among each other in relative harmony. True, the banter got a bit lively on the local newspaper's forum but it wasn't an accurate reflection of how well the various tribes got along.

Around this time, Theodor Herzl, credited as the father of modern Zionism, was campaigning for mass Jewish migration to Palestine to boost efforts to form a Jewish state. In 1902-03 he was invited to give evidence before the *British Royal Commission on Alien Immigration* to support his cause.

During this visit he met Secretary of State for the Colonies Joseph Chamberlain. Joe was a man who made his name in Birmingham, where he launched his political career. He was the mayor of Birmingham for three years and was a successful screw manufacturing magnate.

Joe and Theodor got on famously and Joe promised to pull a few government strings and sort out some kind of settlement for Theodor's extended family.

He asked Egypt if it could spare a patch of land in the Sinai Peninsula for his mate Theodor, but Cairo didn't go for it. So Joe started scouring the map for a bit of British territory no one would mind giving up. He returned to Theodor and said: "Found somewhere. You'll love it, really sunny. It's in East Africa."

The offer of a chunk of Kenya was politely declined by the Zionists — and vehemently opposed by the ex-pats in East Africa.

But importantly, Joe's efforts persuaded the British Government to raise its game in finding a home for the Zionists. And a few years later some Jewish volunteers helped Britain — including, no doubt, some of the Shelby family — in conquering Palestine.

So next time there's an almighty squabble in the Middle East with each side claiming the other one started it, stand up for Birmingham and remind everyone, "Actually, we started that."

Joseph Chamberlain was posthumously awarded the first ever Pride Of Birmingham award in 1958 in recognition of his role in creating the Middle East Problem*.

*[citation needed, for all of it.]

NS

No. 63: Teletext

Before Birmingham gave the world <u>the Internet</u>, information traveled at a much slower and more unreliable pace. Say you were on the terraces of the Spion kop on a Saturday afternoon, depressed, waiting and hoping for some light relief from Billy McNeill's Aston Villa who were probably losing away at Watford. A mention on a round-the-grounds round-up on the radio would filter through the one earpiece of the man with the anorak and transistor, be mumbled to a bloke trying not to stand too close to him, a rumour might become a ripple, would become a gale of laughter — but would it be correct? If you later missed the classified check, you wouldn't really know what had happened until the *Sports Argus* came out — and by that time you were usually a couple of pints on the way to not caring.

Teletext changed all that. Pages around the magic number of 302 would be refreshed feverishly all around the country: from living room to pub. It was a revelation, provided you had a newish telly and a decent signal you could get information in a matter of minutes.

You won't be in the least surprised that it's Birmingham that is responsible for the BREAKING NEWS culture that drowns us, but it's a more circulatory route than some. You can't of course have teletext without television — and a we couldn't have had it if broadcasting television didn't work quite the way it does.

In 1971, Philips (CAL) Laboratories engineer John Adams created a design and proposal for UK broadcasters, which became accepted universally as the basis for all future teletext systems and standards. Eventually it would be established across the globe. Teletext information was broadcast in the vertical blanking interval between image frames in a broadcast television signal: in the gaps between the pictures.

And where do the gaps in between the pictures come from? Guess.

To have gaps, you have to have a series of pictures: those pictures form movement due to something called persistence of vision. Before film, before the What the Butler Saw machines, there was the flip book — the first form of animation to employ a linear sequence of images rather than circular (as in the older phenakistoscope) — and they all work in the same way. The first flip book appeared in September 1868 when it was patented by John Barnes Linnett — a lithographer from Birmingham — under the name kineograph ('moving picture').

From there it's a short hundred or so years until finding out that Graham Turner has been sacked moments after it's happened: thanks to Birmingham and teletext.

These days, when Graham Turner is sacked we just turn to Twitter.

JB

No. 64: Grindcore

You're in a flat-roofed pub you've never been brave
enough to go in before. In the front bar, market workers and bin-men scowl into their pints of Brew XI.
You clutch the photocopied, ransom-note flyer you
picked up in Oasis. You hope the barman doesn't
clock that you're underage. Here, the air is thick
with the reek of smoke, patchouli and pub carpets. A
barrage of drums hits you in the gut. The metallic
skrrangg! of a ferocious guitar cracks your earwax
to make way for permanent tinnitus. Bowel-worry-
ing bass tugs at your nethers. And somewhere in this
unholy mix, a guttural, subhuman bellow brings the
whole congealed mass into something altogether more
primal, more intensely physical than mere music:
GWOOOAAARRGH! This is the best thing ever.

In 1980 two precocious pubescents from the rural
Birmingham suburbs discovered punk. Nic Bullen and
Miles 'Rat' Ratledge became regular penpals with an-
archo-punks Crass and wagged school to get to punk
gigs around the country, crashing in squats, blagging
drinks and generally making a nuisance of themselves.
Of course they formed a band. Everybody did: this
was punk for fuck's sake.

Napalm Death's teen rage at the Thatcher regime and
the urban decay of the post-industrial Midlands was
channelled into the music: the ungodly racket that
became known as grindcore.

Yes it started in pubs, even if they shouldn't have been
in them, and it was 'rock' of a sort, but it was about

as far-removed from the pub-rock origins of London punk as it gets. This shit was real. Napalm Death were so punk that they split up half way through their first proper album. Sides one and two of *Scum* are performed by entirely different groups a year apart, with only deranged, supercharged drummer Mick left to play on both sides.

But that was enough. Already Guinness World Record holders for the shortest recorded song (*You Suffer*: 1 sec) the early Napalm Death members would go on to be some of the most respected, intelligent and influential musicians in alternative music. Justin Broadrick formed Godflesh, spawning industrial metal along the way. Nic and Mick brought dub and techno into the mix with Scorn. And Napalm Death themselves led a new wave of ultra-heavy, super-fast metal punk that evolved, merged with <u>heavy metal</u> (also invented in Brum) and expanded into worldwide genres such as doom metal, black metal and a hundred more, giving generations of moody teenagers all over the world an outlet that was guaranteed to make their parents wonder what on earth they'd done wrong.

If it takes a village to raise a child, it takes a big bad city to raise children like this. You're welcome.

SF

No. 65: Grammar Nazism

Back in 18th century Birmingham's pre-Internet discussion forums, it was harder to get one's kicks by correcting people's misuse of language.

Joseph Priestley — as sort-of hired hand to the Lunar Society — rather had to bite his lip as infinitives were split and modifiers left dangling around the table. James Watt was notorious for announcing he was about to "boldly go and check the plumbing following the meeting" when leaving the dinner table. JP spent so much time fuming at the split infinitive that he never worked out whether there was something dangerously up with the many steam engines that were around, or it was just a euphuism for going to the outdoor privy — and let's not dwell on the engineer's dangling modifier.

Eventually Priestley got so fed up of silently correcting people's grammar that he decided to go public with his pedantry by setting up his own school and publishing *The Rudiments of English Grammar*: pretty much the first ever grammar textbook.

The book was far from the stuffy work one might expect from such a tome and his pupils were treated to many a LOL such as this example of a couplet:

"Beneath this stone my wife doth lie: She's now at rest, and so am I."

Still, the life of a face-to-face grammar nazi has its risks, not only do you have Muphry's Law to contend with, you also risk starting a riot after pointing out "Actually, it's *you're* not allowed to celebrate the storming of the Bastille or we'll torch your house *a lot*".

Not content with riling the illiterate, and getting run out of town, Priestly went on to annoy the superstitious by calling out the bad science behind the nonsense of the theory of the four elements.

Sometimes you just have to thank (the one, singular, unity) God that he didn't live to get a Twitter account.

JG

No. 66: The Hand Grenade

It's possible, but unlikely, that when the kids of today play 'war' they mime sitting in command centres programming drones, or pretend to work on high-level AI routines for infiltrating ISIS on Instagram. It's more likely that they continue to use the main two traditional imaginary weapons: guns and the hand grenade.

We could talk about Birmingham's influence on the gun until the cows come home, but as the cows all live out in Warwickshire barn conversions we'd have to rig up some sort of notification system. So, let's talk grenades, and in particular the famous one known as the Mills Bomb.

The grenade has the same linguistic root as the Spanish for pomegranate ('granada', from the city), so when William Mills developed his bomb at the Mills Munition Factory in Hockley, he chose to shape it very much like a pineapple. It was the first modern fragmentation grenade and was first supplied to our brave boys — and to the imaginations of our little boys — in 1915, which was lucky as there was a war on.

Mills described it as the first "safe grenade", the pin meaning it was safe for the grenadier rather than the grenadee. Well, safe-ish. A good chuck would be in the region of 50 feet, with reasonable accuracy, but the grenade could throw lethal fragments farther than this, so once thrown it was best to take cover.

At first the grenade was fitted with a seven-second fuse, but this delay proved too long and the fuse was reduced to four seconds: it wasn't unknown for targets to pick up a Mills Bomb and send it back where it came from. Well, back to where it was thrown from: it came, as does almost everything worthwhile, from Birmingham.

JB

No. 67: Slapstick Comedy

A number of years ago, during the stag party celebrations for a good friend of mine, I went along to play paintballing.

Upon arrival at the centre we discovered that our opponents for the day were a group of men who had evidently been paintballing on several occasions before. They had the correct footwear, warrior-like nicknames for each other, and most worryingly of all: their own guns. They were likely to be more than a match for our disorganised and hungover group of musicians, liberals and wimps.

And so it proved.

I was 'killed' within 30 seconds of the first game starting, taking a pellet direct to the facemask. My colleagues fared no better. With a mouth full of yellow paint, I watched as my buddies died face-down in the mud. War is hell.

After three or four games, during which we had our arses repeatedly handed to us, the safety official accompanying us around the course became exasperated. "Have any of you ever done this before?", he asked. A single arm was raised, belonging to Richard Loach.

Rich was immediately given the job of captain, which he accepted with some reluctance. He began tentatively, dividing the team into attack and defence squads and muttering something or other about tactics. Soon, however, he began warming to the task and eventually grew visibly before our eyes when he started shouting motivational phrases in a highly animated manner, evoking the spirit of Ron Saunders himself. It was stirring stuff, believe me.

As Rich's speech neared its Henry V climax and, at the very point that we started to believe in ourselves, he shot himself in the foot.

Literally.

A split-second later the hooter honked for the beginning of the next game and the enemy came over the brow of a hill — finding us collapsed in a heap of weeping laughter. They fired at will.

This moment of pure slapstick will live with me forever and a day, and it just so happens that Richard was merely carrying on what is a long Brummie tradition. Without Birmingham, folks, there would be no slapstick comedy.

It really originated with Charlie Hall, who was born in Birmingham in 1899. As a young man he trained as a carpenter before finding his way to <u>Hollywood</u>, via a sister in New York. Working as a stagehand, he became friendly with a young Stan Laurel and eventually appeared in over 40 movies with Stan and his partner-in-LOLs, Oliver Hardy.

During one such film, *The Battle of the Century*, Laurel and Hardy are caught in the middle of a gigantic custard pie fight. This fight was started by none other than Charlie Hall: who threw the first of the 3000 pies.

A Wetherspoons, in his home district of Erdington, is a fitting tribute to a man: where comedy fights are often only a spilt pint away.

Without Birmingham there would be no *You've Been Framed*. Think about that.

As a footnote it is worth mentioning that every child who grew up in Birmingham in the late 1970s and early 1980s went to school with a kid who claimed that his dad was the Phantom Flan Flinger from *Tiswas*. May the circle be unbroken, muckka.

CH

No. 68: Banter

OK, so we're not as proud of this one as some of the others.

'Banter' could have started in a good place: a gentle reminder that some jokes and threads of conversation might be a little morally transgressive, but said amongst friends with the layers of meta-irony and in-jokes they shouldn't be judged alongside other, more public, forms of communication. But that's the trouble with men, generally, we take something good and ruin it for everyone.

You can see where banter comes from. For example, football seems a silly thing in which to invest so much identity and emotion, but it is useful to set men's minds at ease by establishing loose relationships and hierarchies early in a conversation. Men that support Aston Villa claim a higher status because they are a better team, but Birmingham City fans see themselves as more 'authentic'. Now a friendly pantomime can start: each fan casting the other as the foil, with all the appropriate hissing and booing. Thus, everyone has a clear role in the relationship and neither party has to fear making any meaningful or lasting connection, while getting to draw from a wealth of context and years of in-jokes: 'banter'.

The term new lad was coined in 1993, it identified a laddish anti-intellectual backlash to '80s feminism. The strong working class aesthetic of '90s lad culture contrasted sharply to the naked greed and commercialisation that marked the decade before. Not that the commercialisation went away, of course, it's just that the new lads were sold things that had few of the trappings of class aspiration: limited edition tracksuits and designer T-shirts replaced Italian suits and handmade shoes.

The label that brought expensive T-shirts to every high street and football terrace was French Connection. In 1991 a slogan was born, the idea developed by Birmingham-born Trevor Beattie. Soon every dull lad disciple was paying over odds for plain black fitted T-shirts with such slogans as 'Fcuk fashion' or 'Too busy to fcuk' or 'My friend's tight expensive T-shirt is making me want to gently fcuk him while he sleeps'. I made the last one up: it would never have been made because it was genuinely transgressive.

In the same half of this decade Beattie would, through some judo flip of zeitgeist mastery, use lad culture to sell Wonderbras to women. The famous 'Hello Boys' of Eva Herzigova, the idealised woman of lad culture.

Both campaigns caused uproar, column inches, a snarky comment from a judge, and traffic accidents that turned out to be entirely fictional. Of course the reaction to the disapproval was: 'You just don't get it'. The same reaction that any criticism of the bantering lads today will get.

In this case, however, it was probably fair: the transgressions were no more extreme than slightly unclothed breasts, *almost* a rude word and non-existent collisions. But after 20 years of the same attitude, each attempt to shock in the name of free speech and standing up for the under-represented white male growing ever more racist, sexist or just plain moronic this othering of critics has developed into the concept of banter. And that's the essential problem with the term banter: it shifts the blame from the actor to the viewer, it's an umbrella from responsibility to a type of person who doesn't really believe in free speech, they want the luxury of being offensive with no conse-quences.

Sorry.

DS

No. 69: Nerds

Pretty much anyone who ever invented or discovered anything of note was a nerd.

Just look around you: electronic devices; carpet; the shoes on your feet. All of those things, just like everything else man has created, from the world-changing discoveries to the mundane, everyday items, only exist in the first place because someone, somewhere had an idea and then worked obsessively to make it a reality.

In other words, someone was sufficiently nerdy about it to will it into being.

You'd think, then, that we'd celebrate the nerd. You'd think that the state of nerd-dom, the practice of nerd-ery, the act of nerding, would be highly prized. You'd think it would be something to aspire to, but it isn't. It's quite the opposite, in fact. Let's look at the diction-ary definition.

> Nerd (noun: informal) 1. a foolish or contemptible person who lacks social skills or is boringly studious. 2. a single-minded expert in a particular technical field.

Thomas Edison, Albert Einstein and Marie Cu-rie were all nerds by that second definition, and all are quite rightly held in high esteem by our culture. Chances are, though, that when you read the word 'Nerd' at the top of this article the picture that formed in your head was based not on the invention of the lightbulb, or the theory or relativity, or the fight against cancer, but was instead based on that pejorative first definition.

Not only that, but it's also likely that the mental image your mind effortlessly conjured up is one that is very similar to the image many others would have arrived at. This is because it is a mental image that is deeply informed by popular culture: The Comic Book Guy from *The Simpsons*; Moss from *The IT Crowd*; Egon Spengler from *Ghostbusters* — socially awkward weirdos who will never, ever get laid. The customers of Nostalgia and Comics. Nerds.

These types of nerd, rather than the cancer-curing, electric light-giving nerd, have a particular function in our society: They are there to make you feel better about your own obsessions. Nerds are effectively a barometer of cool and sit firmly on the bottom rung in the social caste system. No-one wants to be a nerd.

But, and here's the thing, we're ALL nerds.

We're all nerds because we're all barking mad in one way or another and to varying degrees — we all have something (or more than one thing) that is our 'thing'. Running, cooking, shopping, DIY, gardening — you name it and I'll show you someone who is a little bit more into it than most.

My particular 'thing' is Pop Music and, as luck would have it, society deems that to be 'quite cool'. My mate Robson's 'thing' is poetry, and society deems that to be 'quite interesting'. I'm sure your 'thing' is also an equally interesting and sexy 'thing'. Well done, you.

If, however, your 'thing' happens to be science fiction, or computer games, or comics, or — heaven forbid — all three, well, you're fucked. You are a first definition nerd, you sad sack. Guess what? This brutal social and cultural apartheid in which all of Western culture blithely takes part would not be possible without the city of Birmingham!

It was here, in 1971, that the first meeting of the Birmingham Science Fiction Group took place. Initially the BSFG met informally in pubs and acted as a space where Science Fiction fans could discuss their 'thing' with like-minded individuals, but it soon evolved into a proper organisation with members all over the world and laid the groundwork for a network of other organisations that grew throughout the 1980s and beyond, all of which ultimately cemented the idea of the nerd-as-saddo in the collective consciousness.

So, next time you see some poor, geeky kid getting his head stuck down the bog in an American movie, remember that such mindless and arbitrary persecution started right here in Brum, bab.

CH

No. 70: The Kitchen-Sink Modernist Novel

Two o'clock, 1929, Tyseley, Birmingham, Henry Green walked Warwick Road, near current DFS, Foam Cut to Size, Hollywood Monster.

Standing in Tyseley, son of Mr Yorke, thought in mind and it seemed to him that these factories were beautiful and he reached out feeling to them and he touched them; he thought only in Birmingham now was honesty left for in the county and Oxford and Eton, in society, words were like sheep while here men created what you could touch, soft like silk, flowing without definite article, which would last, although not as well as those of contemporary Orwell or Oxford tutor C.S. Lewis.

He thought, he declaimed to himself, this was life to lead, making useful modernist novels that were beautiful, and glad for making them, which you could touch; but when he was most sure he remembered. He remembered how it has all been said before and experience of father's bottling factory became basis for great work of modernism; first to use working class experience. And then what had been so plain, stiff and bursting inside him like pumps at Mermaid on Stratford Rd, died like fun at Acock's Green Wetherspoons, and he felt embarrassed standing as he did in fine clothes.

JB — with apologies to Henry Green's great modernist masterpiece Living *which is set in Tyseley.*

No. 71: Bono

Paul David Hewson, better known as Bono, the lead singer of U2, is arguably the most unpopular internationally successful rock star millionaire the world has ever seen. His story is a weird contradiction. On the one hand, he has sold millions of records and filled enormodomes across the globe during a career that has spanned more than 30 years, but, on the other, he really, really, really boils a lot of peoples' piss.

In fact, the only other fabulously successful musician who runs him even close is Sting, with his lute and his tantric sex. But even Sting knows that he walks very much in Bono's shadow.

Younger pop models can't really hold a candle to Bono and Sting in these terms, although it's true that Thom Yorke is busy making a fist of playing catch up. Radiohead, however, remain very much a parochial concern in comparison to the behemoths of U2 and Sting.

There are a lot of reasons why Bono might get on people's nerves: the out-of-place histrionics on the Band Aid single, his tax efficiency, the poncing about onstage with a flag, his apparently pivotal role in the Northern Irish peace process, the shades worn indoors at all times, the unanswered questions about the AIDS charities he endorses, the disappointment that follows when one misreads his name as 'Boon', that appeal video where he clicks his fingers, and, of course, the music he makes.

A more interesting question, however, would be one that could help us understand what makes him tick. Whether you love, loathe or are entirely ambivalent about U2, their ability to stay at or near the top for so long is admirable, and to achieve that you must surely need a deep-seated desire and personal drive. Where does that come from, Bono?

One answer might be found in the Bible, from Luke 4:24: "And he said, "Truly, I say to you, no prophet is acceptable in his hometown", because this nugget of wisdom is particularly true in the case of Bono.

Despite being partly responsible for making millions of people around the world aware of the fact that Dublin is a vibrant musical city, and despite building U2's recording studio and base of operations in the city, at a time when they could easily have relocated to New York, London or LA, and despite, even, paving the way for The Script to annoy the beejesus out of the English, the fact remains that the majority of Dubliners think Bono is a bollix and a pox. And he knows it, and that must really gall him. No, Dublin and Dubliners have not taken Bono to their hearts. Possibly this is for some of the reasons outlined above. Mainly, however, it's because the rock and roll part of Dublin's hearts is already and forever occupied. Dublin, you see, is very much Phil Lynott's town.

Lynott's hard rocking, hard drinking lifestyle, and his re-workings of rebel songs — most notably *Whisky In The Jar* — took his band, Thin Lizzy, into the stratosphere during the 1970s, and his romantic/tragic death at the tender age of 36, all combine to make him the ideal, classic, rock and roll hero. Since 1987, Dublin has held an annual music festival in his honour and, in 2005, the city erected a life-size bronze statue. In it's description of the statue on their official site, the Visit Dublin tourist board describe Lynott as 'Dublin's most beloved musical son'. Poor old Bono.

It's a little known fact, however, that Phil Lynott is actually a Brummie. Phil's parents met in Birmingham in the late 1940s and had a short relationship. His father, Cecil Parris, had moved away to London by the time his mother, Phyliss Lynott, discovered that she was pregnant. After Phil was born in Sandwell hospital, and this being 1949 — a time less enlightened time, shall we say — they were moved into a home for un-married mothers on the Raddlebarn Road in Selly Park (the building still stands, but is now St Mary's Hospice). Phil was later christened at St Edwards Church, just across the road from the home, and his formative years were spent here as a Brummie before, following a very brief stay in plucky little <u>Manchester</u>, Phil went to live with his Grandmother in Crumlin, Dublin, and the rest is Bono-baiting history.

Incidentally, Thin Lizzy's big break came following a tour support with local heroes, Slade, during which Lynott took inspiration from Noddy Holder's top hat to adorn his bass guitar with mirrors… but that's another story.

So, next time Mr Hewson appears on your telly, radio, or completely uninvited in your iTunes library, just remember that it all started right here.   *- CH*

No. 72: The Great British Worker

Stalwart vessels of early <u>British satire</u>, Ronald Barker and Ronald Corbett had a fine line in jokes about the perceived work ethic of the country's factory fodder. "An aerial photograph of the track at British Leyland," they announced, "was spoilt when somebody moved."

You see, it had become an establishment trope that the car workers of Britain — and those in Longbridge, Birmingham in particular — were not industrious and prone to stoppage. That was of course untrue, the workers of those car plants were hard-working: not a house in Birmingham wasn't freshly painted in Mini green at least once a year.

But there was media and establishment bias against the workers of Longbridge, and that was often focused on one man: Derek 'Red Robbo' Robinson, of North-field (you wouldn't want to live too far from where you worked in those days, the cars were terribly unreliable).

Born in 1927, Robinson started work there during the height of the Second World War and joined the Amalgamated Engineering Union (now lost in a midst of mergers like most left wing organisations). The political situation at work was very different then, the Communist Party dominated the factory's workforce, and many hundreds of Daily Workers were sold there every day.

You can imagine the lads on their tea break, talking about last night's game (and Birmingham City were often on top in wartime football) when one holds up a page three essay on the theories of Antonio Gramsci. "Phwoar, eh lads? Look at the critique of bourgeoise hegemony on that."

You might think that the bosses have a lot of weight behind them these days, but in the late '70s the real boss was the real establishment: the government. Nationalisation (in 1975) ensured that any futures disputes could be framed by politicians and the papers as not just bad for business, but bad for Britain.

The creatives back then were more Austin 7s and ermine robes than flannel shirts and fixies. Leonard Lord, the designer of the Mini, which was Longbridge's main output, became Baron Lambury of Northfield. Although it can't have been much fun in the House of Lords being Baron of Northfield, imagine having to explain that, yes, there is game and shooting on your estate, but not a huge amount of grouse.

When Derek Robinson, by then trade union convenor, took on the management he was taking on both the Commons and the Lords. But he was used to large odds, having stood as a Communist candidate in four consecutive general elections in Northfield between 1966 and 1974 (he lost his deposit on each occasion).

Whilst it's true that the company lost a lot of cars and money through strike action, what ended up being the real problem was the effect that the strikes — mediated through the news establishment — had on the public's perception of the company and the cars it made. British Leyland began to symbolise all that was supposedly wrong with Britain, what we were told the rest of the world was calling the 'English Disease' — which would seem a bit rich, especially from the French.

The narrative became that, alongside the strikes there was a marked decline in build quality, for which the unions and the workers were blamed. Brummie craftsmanship was now being called into question, with 'a Brummagem screwdriver' becoming a poor comedian's unwitty euphemism for a hammer.

The story goes that he was getting in the way of the company's preparations to bring the new Austin Metro into production, probably the only thing on which he would ever see eye-to-eye with Jeremy Clarkson. Longbridge was being redeveloped and heavily automated, there would be job losses and Derek wouldn't stand for that.

MD Sir Michael Edwardes admitted, "The answer is 'Yes', from a strategic point of view we knew that we couldn't have the Metro and him." Robinson was eventually sacked by British Leyland in 1979.

Taking on the management took guts, but Robbo had to contend with Spooks too. At the time of his dismissal one of his union officials was rumoured to be in the pay of M15. You may think this sounds plausible, we couldn't possibly comment.

Derek Robinson has been credited with causing 523 walk-outs at Longbridge between 1978 and 1979, costing an estimated £200m in lost production. So next time the media talk about productivity losses caused by an early football kick off or some inclement weather, pay tribute to Red Robbo: a great British worker, strong enough to take on the establishment, and a Brummie to boot.

JB

No. 73: The 45th President of the USA

On Tuesday, 8 November, 2016 voters in the USA will choose their 45th President. If it's not Hillary then Hillary will at least be the story. Behind every great woman is a man, and behind that man is a song, and behind that song is a woman, and that woman is from Bearwood. Behind which is: Birmingham.

The song that catapulted Bill Clinton to the presidency was *Don't Stop* by Fleetwood Mac: a hopeful song forged in adultery, a message between two parts of a powerful professional couple whose careers were intertwined.

Don't Stop was written by Christine McVie who grew up in Bearwood, the daughter of a concert violinist and music teacher. She studied art in Birmingham and played in bands, getting connected within the music scene. Her own career was going pretty well but it wasn't until she met and married John McVie, and then joined his band Fleetwood Mac, that she really found success. Both partners to the marriage found greater success during their period of professional and marital partnership then they had before, peaking with *Rumours* the album that gave us *Don't Stop* — Bill's election theme and the tour that preceded the McVie's divorce.

McVie has said that the song is about her feelings around the break-up of their marriage. She'd also written another song on the album about how much she was enjoying her affair with Fleetwood Mac's lighting director, this might seem bastardly behaviour but it was pretty standard in the Mac at the time. Christine, being an honest Brummie type, at least wasn't as bad as Lyndsey Buckingham whose contemporary practise was to write songs about how he didn't love partner Stevie Nicks: and then give them to her to sing. This author likes to cast her in the role of Bill and so we look again at the lyrics, hopeful but also personal, a love letter to Hillary perhaps:

"Don't stop, thinking about tomorrow, Don't stop, it'll soon be here, It'll be, better than before, Yesterday's gone, yesterday's gone.

Don't you look back, Don't you look back."

What's next? Hillary in 2016, that's what.

JH

No. 74: Handwriting

Do you do little loops at the bottom of your y's? Do you draw little hearts over the top of your i's? Do you, when actually pressed to use a pen at all after years of typing and texting, get all flummoxed and end up using block capitals so at least people have a fighting chance of understanding you? Well, you'll never guess, Birmingham is responsible for that.

Y'see back in the 19th century people used quills for writing, it was a splodgy, blotty, ink-stained business. You had to be skilled and neat, you couldn't develop your own style very much. But then John Mitchell, down in Newhall Street, pioneered mass production of steel pens and suddenly writing just became a bit easier.

Soon thousands of people and dozens of companies were using Birmingham to make pens of different sizes and quality and the city gave easy communication to the world. And that lasted until a few years ago, because loads of us just don't pick up a pen very often any more — and even the prime minister uses text speak. LOL.

Lots of love.

JB

No. 75: Airside Shopping

There's a place at the airport that they call 'airside'. It used to be called 'the departure lounge' but that suggests you're leaving soon and you're not, really you're not.

The amount of time that we spend airside seems to go up year by year, increasing at a faster rate than the processor power increases on new computer chips. It really needs a 'law' — and, considering it seems like you are stuck in a place that pretends to be holiday when it is not, maybe we can call it 'Keith Barron's Law'.

Whilst we have the response to existential threats of terrorism to *blame* for this it really couldn't have all happened without Birmingham.

You see, the reason why we have to get ourselves to the airport so far in advance of our flight is so that we can be screened — for bombs, nail clippers, bottles of water and moisturiser. The fact that we are processed and dumped airside swiftly is just a happy quirk of the system that works very well for the small town of traders we find in what once was 'departures'. And we wouldn't get airside so quickly were it not for the x-ray, invented here in Birmingham in 1896 by Major John Hall Edwards.

There are many applications of the x-ray, but none are quite so profitable as their use in airport security to screen our bags, and increasingly our bodies too. It's the x-ray that gets us into the airside mall with hours to spare; precious hours in which we can enjoy the unique shopping experience. And what an experience it is, friends. For here, airside, we find high street names trading with 'gotcha' mark-ups on all the essentials that you couldn't bring through the security checks: deodorant, water, toothpaste. They've also seen you coming and know you've forgotten socks or pants so those are heavily marked up too. And once you have done all the emergency shopping you can manage there's still time for a burger and a pint deal, again charged above the going rate.

Next, take in the 'duty free shopping' area. Here you'll find a bewildering arrangement of 'airport exclusives' — products that you can't buy on the high street at all, so you can't tell if they're actually a bargain or not. Finally, if you still have time to kill, you can enter the raffle to win a high performance sports car — something which can only be done airside. This truly is the land of opportunities, and I for one am glad of Birmingham, glad of the x-ray, glad that I got here with time to spare.

Now then, I need to grab some spare socks…

JH

No. 76: New Coke

Americans hated New Coke. Scared by loss of market share to Pepsi, The Coca-Cola Company decided in 1985 to reformulate and relaunch their particular brand of sugary mess. As it turned out people don't like change, and this played even more into Pepsi's hands.

One chap in New Mexico reportedly stockpiled a thousand dollars worth of 'old coke', drinkers were revolting. And their teeth were dissolving. Southern USA-ians considered the drink a fundamental part of regional identity and viewed the company's decision to change the formula through the prism of the Civil War, as another surrender to the Yankees — which is about the standard of reasoned debate you see in American politics today.

It's the biggest **PR** disaster in business history — and Coke soon returned to 'classic' — just be glad we didn't have hordes of social media consultants blogging on the lessons we could all learn from it.

You shouldn't mess with fizzy pop. And fizzy pop, as any fool knows was created by the Birmingham Lunar Society member Joseph Priestley as he worked on isolating Oxygen from the rest of air — presumably as that was thirsty work. Priestley published a paper called *Directions for Impregnating Water with Fixed Air* in 1772, which explained how to make soda water. I haven't read it but assume it can be paraphrased as "put normal water in a Soda Stream".   *-JB*

No. 77: Words

We are dismayed quarterly, when the *Oxford English Dictionary* appears to show no restraint in adding the latest fad neologisms, such as 'selfie' (not to be confused with any photo of a person), 'hashtag' (not to be confused with the hash symbol), and 'flexitarian' (not to be confused with a word you can say without sounding like an idiot). Although it did take them until this year to add Blu-Tack as both a noun and a verb. I Blu-Tack, you Blu-Tack, he Blu-Tacks, she Blu-Tacks… You never see white tack any more do you?

Well all these 'orrible abbreviations, port-manteaux, and proprietary eponyms are kind of our fault, for which we are truly sorry, aka sozzlebobbles (probably). We may not like them, but words are all [we] have, as those Bee Gees might have said.

Back in the early 18th Century, a fella named Thomas Warren opened a bookshop on the High Street. He also decided to publish Birmingham's first weekly newspaper, the Birmingham Journal. In response to his Brummie colleagues' spelling and grammar fails, one of the contributing journos, pedant Samuel Johnson, went on to write one of the first ever diction-aries of the English language, called *A Dictionary of the English Language*. It was "one of the greatest single achievements of scholarship" and "among the most influential dictionaries in the history of the English language".

Sadly, it hasn't improved the standards of our local press.   -*JG*

No. 78: Running a Marathon

In 2014 running is a spectacle and it's a big business. The Great North Run and the London Marathon are sporting mega-events: televised and commodified, they're about much more than running. They're about cities, landmarks, tourism, charity, personal achievements, narratives and mythology. Ultimately they are about ways of constructing those things for us and about controlling the meaning of them.

The London Marathon constructs achievement in a particular way: completing the distance of the run, attaining the sponsorship required if you are taking a charity place, and then performing all of this in a specific place in the service both of an officially sanctioned view of London and of a corporate sponsor. Looked at through my cynical eyes, runners in the London Marathon are extras in the service of this year's sponsor (currently Virgin Money) and of the Mayor of London because the most significant and persistent symbols we see in the televised coverage of the race are the sponsor's logo and the landscape of the city: the runners are just a device that drives the story, and that provide a frame for the more important messages of our sponsors.

Now, I acknowledge that the runners enjoy their day and gain a lot of personal benefit from their experience. I wouldn't want to detract from anyone's achievements. I just wonder if this all couldn't happen another way. You see, it used to be very different, back when Birmingham invented the big city marathon.

On May 31st 1980 *Athletics Weekly* claimed that:

"In years to come, when marathon fields several thousand strong will be commonplace in Britain, it will be seen that the event which triggered off the mass long-distance running movement in this country was the inaugural People's Marathon"

And where did the People's Marathon take place? Birmingham of course, where it ran from 1980-1985, pre-dating the Great North Run and the London Marathon.

The People's Marathon was something of a détournement, a political intervention in the otherwise elitist world of long distance running: founder John Walker wanted to open up the world of marathon running to the masses, those who were not athletes but who were interested in working towards a challenging goal — hence the name, the People's Marathon. It's ironic then that the establishment responded by recuperating mass participation running, taking back control of the marathon agenda and turning it into an advert for polyunsaturated margarines, private medical care, and Internet banking. For the essence of John's idea exists in all the major events, including our own Birmingham Half Marathon (sorry, the Bupa Birmingham Great Run), but it has been pulled back into the spectacle. The challenge that the People's Marathon set is still there and the open call for participation is too, what is missing is character, what's missing is the political intent which is lost in the tightly regulated world of the run as a mega-event.

Modern running events rely on an artificial scarcity for their existence. I've often seen friends disappointed that they have missed out on a place for the (Virgin Money) London Marathon or the (Bupa) Great North Run as if their personal narrative of running is invalid unless it is mediated through one of these televised events, and that saddens me. I understand the desire to enjoy running in an atmosphere and the need to have a tangible target to work towards but I wonder if we can't achieve those things in a new way.

At the end of the day there is nothing to stop us from running when we want to run, but we have allowed ourselves to be tricked into believing that we need authorities to grant us permission to do so. There are signs that this is beginning to change.

In 2014 the Sheffield Half Marathon was officially cancelled moments before its planned start time because the organisers had failed to provide water to the water stations. The people of Sheffield, already assembled in their lycra, ran the race anyway. They realised that the roads were public realm, they realised that you can always find 13 miles to run, and you didn't need an authority to tell you to do that.

Then we have the race-crasher, the bandit: the runner who doesn't register but turns up and uses their right of access to the public road during a sanctioned race.

With our modern technology, GPS watches and phones, we could run a distance course whenever we want because our devices help us to plan and measure a route. I have a half-marathon route home from work that I run several times a year. Sure it's not a race but if all I want to do is hit a personal milestone, why tie myself to Bupa's calendar and wait until October for the official Birmingham Half? Groups like Parkrun are adding levels of organisation to this by staging runs around the world on a regular basis and pooling the results to create a sort of glocalised mega-event. My personal favourite intervention into this space is the Run Free Race which asks people from around the world to spoof a mass participation running race by flooding their social networks with images from imaginary races that they are holding on their own terms.

I think there is a new psychogeography of running emerging. I call it the unrun: running on your own terms, running to construct your own meanings, pushing back and putting John Walker's idea of people back into running.

Eric Langford ran the 1980 People's Marathon and was interviewed recently by the BBC. "There was nothing to compare it with," he said, "we went on the M42 before it was opened. We were making our amusement as we went along I think." That's what Birmingham gave the world: running for exploration, running to reclaim space. There is footage of the People's Marathon online and it seems playful and free. Its route isn't bogged down with landmarks and touristic symbolism, it's a jog around the city from Chelmsley Wood that uses a half-built motorway out of curiosity and pragmatism. So what happened to the People's Marathon? "Everyone wanted a piece of the action." (Eric Langford again) "London came along. And it was on the telly…" And so the spectacle triumphed once more. But that was then. We could be at a tipping point now. Let's not wait for 'them' to give us back our marathon, let's just get out there and run when and where we want. Did you know that if you ran the 11 Route then that is pretty much a marathon? You do now.

Jog on Birmingham.

JH

No. 79: The Ironing

Back in the days before anything was open on a Sunday, the gentleman of the house would repair at noon to the local hostelry and return home pie-eyed at about half past two. He'd then sleep off his roast dinner in an armchair, before it was time for *That's Life* and then bed.

For his adoring wife there was but one thing to do: iron his clothes for the week ahead in front of a black and white film. As Bette Davis wept to a finale, the shirts would pile up neatly folded on the sofa. And this picture of everyday sexist bliss was brought to you by the city of Birmingham.

In 1722 Richard Baddeley, an ironmonger of this parish, patented a method for casting wheel streaks and box irons. Whatever wheel streaks are is best left to history, but a box iron is a type of clothes iron. The base is a container, into which are put coals or a metal brick to keep the iron hot.

Before this irons were wrought by hand, not so smooth, and prone to causing all sorts of snagging: causing frustrated wife, causing mild cursing, resulting in rousal of a snoozing husband. And that would never do. Not until it was time for at least *One Man and His Dog*.

Birmingham: cause of domestic bliss since 1722.

JB

No. 80: An Inferiority Complex

Sometimes we all feel like we're just not worthy of attention: even though we are perfectly fine women, men, and cities. We share the experience of being unable to reach a subconscious, illusionary, final goal of subjective security and success to compensate for the feelings of inadequacy. If we're not careful we may exhibit an inferiority complex.

Stemming from the psychoanalytic branch of psychology, the concept of the inferiority complex is one of Sigmund Freud's. Alfred Adler, founder of classical Adlerian psychology, held that many neurotic symptoms could be traced to overcompensation for this feeling — like building a big bed-spring-style library when there is already a perfectly good one less than a hundred yards away, for example. Or shovelling visitors between antiseptic hotel and featureless conference centre without letting them see the real city. Or rebranding over and again (the PR equivalent of stuffing shuttlecocks down our collective pants).

But who are we comparing ourselves to? Surely a city as well appointed and industrious should be confident in its place in the world. Size may not be everything but we're carrying a pretty package.

Further analysis reveals the source of all anxiety: in 1890 a professor of physics at Mason Science College (now the University of Birmingham) called John Henry Poynting calculated the mass of the Earth and forever made us all feel small and insignificant.

Perhaps, before that date, Brummies were as annoying overconfident and gobby as Cockneys and those from Greater Manchester. But now we have a lovely line in self deprecation — like good people everywhere — thank Birmingham and Prof Poynting, and thank heaven and earth, for that.

JB

No. 81: The Second (and Third, and so on) Iraq Wars

I was watching *Sportsnight*, or possibly *Midweek Sports Special*, when the first Iraq war really kicked off. It was the 17th January 1991 and the star attraction on the late night TV show was the Football League Cup fifth round tie between Chelsea and Spurs. Dennis Wise was scuttling around the midfield, about to swing a shin at a loose ball, when all of a sudden there was a flash of light.

The stadium appeared to go dark, lines and movement were picked out only in a flickering glow. The floodlights were not white, but green — I would later find out when I watched again on a colour TV — and were picking out not the misplaced passes of Andy Townsend and John Bumstead but laser guided US Tomahawk Cruise Missiles.

I'd dozed off for a second and coverage of the game had been replaced with live action — of the start of 'Stormin' Norman' Schwarzkopf's bombardment of Baghdad.

They never showed the end of the game. I don't know who won. They haven't shown much on telly since, apart from different versions of mainly America and usually 'us' bombing the fuck out of some part of the Middle East. The first Iraq war begat the second, and the second begat the third, and still it begets, much like the famous literature of that general region. And it begets because of oil, and money, and power and because of war-mongering bastards like Tony Blair. But it also begets because it looks good on TV, and it looks good on TV because of Birmingham.

Back in 1918 Oliver Lucas's company — Lucas's to any Brummie — really got working on the military search light and the British forces were able to "create 'artificial moonlight' to enhance opportunities for night attacks". That practise continued, for many years, but it wasn't until the days of rolling news that it became a form of infrared entertainment. An entertainment too good to resist sequel after sequel, whatever the quality.

I've just looked up the result of the game: it was 0-0. And that couldn't be more apt if it were a metaphor.

It *was* a metaphor, guess where they were invented?

JB

No. 82: Dieting

Essentially it's eating less food, so how is dieting a huge industry around the world? Heinz (the <u>HP</u>-stealing bastards) produce special 'Weight Watchers' foods, supposedly healthy versions of their TV dinners. Here's the rub: the main way they contain less calories is by having less food. And they cost more. For less. See what they're doing to you here?

The king of diet food, as opposed to amusing Barry Bethel promoted food replacement food like Slim Fast, is Ryvita. Rough to the eyes, rough to the tongue and rough to the tastebuds, Ryvita is the most diet-y of diet food. And that's how we do things in this country.

In Scandinavia, they just thought it was normal food — the jumper-wearing, murdering, alfresco sex, fools. It took Birmingham to see its potential as food you didn't really want to eat but bought and ate because it was fewer calories than the food you wanted to. Having seen crispbread abroad Englishman Camp-bell-Garratt opened his Ryvita factory in Birmingham in 1925 and the rest is history.

Literally, in terms of the factory, as the Germans bombed the heck out of it during the war. One could almost understand.

JB

No. 83: The Beatles

The Beatles, when they started, were not much more than a bunch of pretty boys with guitars. And guitars were going out of fashion. The band were popular, but may well have slunk out of cultural history in the same way as, for example, The Applejacks — if it wasn't for *Sgt Pepper*. It's routinely named as the greatest album of all time in every list known to man, but the real glue that holds this album together is not George, Ringo, John and Paul's playing, writing or vivid imagination but the Brummie legend that is the mellotron.

Made by Bradmatic Ltd of Aston, Birmingham, the mellotron was an odd looking contraption that chimed with Brum's long held unofficial title of 'a city of a thousand trades' by being the first instrument of '18 sounds' greatly expanding the possibilities of musical hippies, svengalis and The Moody Blueses, the world over.

In a complex operation, one that could only have been conceived by the genius minds of Brummies exposed to the daily intake of the fumes of the HP Sauce factory across the road, the mellotron allowed musicians to have 18 'instruments' at the touch of their fingertips. Their right fingertips, on the right keyboard had lead 'instruments' like strings, flutes and brass and the left fingertips, on the left keyboard had pre-recorded musical rhythm tracks in various styles.

This was a whole new world for music visionary Mike Pinder of The Moody Blues who happened to work at the company (now called Streetly Electronics) and would pave the way for Mike to create smash chart toppers like *Nights In White Satin*.

Mike introduced Lennon and McCartney to the wonders of the mellotron, impressing them with tales of how Peter Sellers, L.Ron Hubbard, King Hussein and Princess Margaret all owned one and how they would gather their respective families around them and amaze with the weird sounds they could conjure up in the name of art.

Suitably impressed The Beatles bought one not wanting to be left behind in the ever increasing influence of the mellotron musicians circle. They dabbled with the mellotron on the little ditty *Tomorrow Never Knows* from *Revolver* before accepting the inevitable and wholeheartedly committing to using it on their next LP: *Sgt Pepper*.

The mellotron is notable in its use on *Strawberry Fields Forever* and *Lovely Rita* but it was the freedom to experiment that was to be the mellotron's greatest gift to the fabs. *Sgt Pepper* ushered in the Summer of Love and the explosion in psychedelic rock music.

Seeing the success that the mellotron had brought for the likeable, although by now slightly grizzled, Scousers, rock stars from across the world looked for some of that mellotron magic to be sprinkled on their otherwise dull music.

JC

No. 84: Saving the World from Climate Change

On the last day of October 2014, as trick or treaters took to the streets of the city suburbs for Halloween-themed fun, something genuinely terrifying was in the air.

It wasn't the fact that Halloween has become, over the last few years, a poster child for the creeping Americanisation of our culture. Nor was it the fact that, just like the manner in which we've all apparently just rolled over and accepted that 'High School Proms' are now a thing, or that it's OK for the FA Cup Final to kick off at 5.30pm, that we just don't seem to have the energy to fight this kind of bullshit anymore.

It wasn't even that we allow the economic machine to hijack dates on our calendar as merely points at which they can market disposable plastic shite to us.

Nor was it the fact that we not only buy this stuff, but that we then chuck it away — even though we know we'll be buying the same plastic shite at precisely the same time again next year.

And it wasn't even that the only thing that differentiates one plastic shite sales opportunity from the next one is how one now 'naturally' follows the other in a never-ending cycle, with the end of Halloween simply firing the starting pistol on Christmas, and so on.

I'm struck by the fact, as I sit here in my Levi jeans, and my Adidas trainers, writing this Marxist claptrap on an Apple laptop like the massive liberal hypocrite that I am, that, depressing as it is, none of the above is actually the truly scary thing about Halloween 2014.

No, the truly scary and depressing thing about the evening of the last day of October 2014, on a traditionally cold and rainy island in the Northern hemisphere, was that the temperature was 19 degrees Celsius at 7.30pm. That's T-shirt weather.

Many people commented about this in online forums such as Twitter and Facebook. As it should have been cold but was actually hot, yeah, many people made jokey, gallows humour comments along the lines of "Global Warming may not be such a bad thing LOL".

Human beings are, as usual, probably laughing their arses off all the way to oblivion, because if and when Global Warming, or Climate Change as it is also known, does come to bite us on our collective arse, the laughing will surely stop.

The amount of planet's carbon resources we can safely use is running out, and we're the only species on earth that is likely to use those remaining resources at an even faster rate in an attempt to stop other sections of the species having access to the rapidly depleting resources. We'd use our last gallon of oil to blow something up, rather than create a shelter. We're that dumb.

Yes, Climate Change will probably do for us all in the end, and then the planet will heave a sigh of relief.

We'll leave behind, amongst other things, millions and millions of plastic orange buckets with scary faces painted on them.

Now, it's fair to point out that the process of efficiently digging things out of the ground and then burning them in order to make other things that will then be disposed of and end up being buried in the ground, and all on a massive scale, started right here in Birmingham with the Industrial Revolution. So the problem of Climate Change is sort of our fault. Sorry about that. But that's not what this entry is about.

What this entry is about is the spark of understanding that might save us all. And that inspiration is also a Brummie thing.

The first realisation of what we we've been doing to the planet, and thus the start of a potential change in our collective behaviour, also started right here in this city. World-renowned palaeoentomologist, Russell Coope (1930-2011), was Professor of Quaternary Science at the University of Birmingham until his retirement in 1993. In the late 1950s, he discovered fossil beetle remains in an organic layer recovered from a quarry, and found that some of the beetles came from warm periods, whilst others came from extremely cold periods. Going against the academic and scientific orthodoxy of the time, Coope proved that occasional changes in climate were extremely abrupt, a theory which was eventually adapted in studies of the Greenland ice cores, from which we learned about the causes and effects of Climate Change.

We gave the world a massive problem, and then we gave it the tools to fix it, if only the world would choose to listen.

CH

No. 85: Ironic Sexism

Birmingham is synonymous with a certain type of Modernism. The square concrete type, formed of square concrete forms, copulating with the sky. Let's call it Brutalism, not only because it's its name, but because in its ambition and its scale — and in an early Red Dwarf sense — it is brutal.

Some cities invent architectural movements, others have them thrust right up them. Birmingham is the latter, although through the inverted prism of our own John Madin we have seen some of its great thrustings.

Modernism thrived at a time when the world, or at least a few square miles of London, became alive with possibilities and freedom. Freedom that, as it radiated around the Hanger Lane gyratory, thrown centrifugally out to the provinces, became new possibilities for oppressing and objectifying women.

Some fought back. Feminism eventually made strides, feminists wore strides (and dungarees). But before political correctness could triumph, there was a high water mark. And all it took was one man to stand idle. With a camera. And one woman's tennis skirt to have a high mark of its own: way above the sporting plimsoll line.

That man was Martin Elliott, that woman his then girlfriend Fiona Walker, and that tennis court was round the back of a University of Birmingham. Not more than a couple of miles from where the game was invented (tennis, not sexism).

The resulting poster sold in the millions. The glimpse of sun behind the rising moon shedding light on the fact that, yes, the occupant of this student room or bedsit was indeed an arse. And not an attractive one.

But let's, *Shawshank*-style, peel back the poster and the covers on these spunk-stained cells and look twenty years into the future to about 1996. A future where this sort of objectification was not on. A future where, in law at least, the woman was equal.

And then culture found a way. Under the guise of postmodernism (no Brummies, not The Mailbox) suddenly that sort of sexism was alright again. You see, in the '90s, it became possible to be and arse and a tit with impunity: as long as you said the pictures on your wall of the same were enjoyed ironically.

Members of Oasis and Paul Weller fans across the country could simultaneously display "that picture of the tennis bird scratching her arse" and get away with it in the eyes of the *NME*. And, like the rise of Ocean Colour Scene, it was both ineffable and all due to Birmingham.

JB

No. 86: Prog Rock

The history of popular music is the story of youth, sex, drugs and revolution.

It's also the story of the ruthless exploitation of naïve young dreamers by savage and unscrupulous media professionals, a long process of vertical integration by global entertainment conglomerates, and the development, packaging, and marketing of products to carefully constructed and controlled sets of audiences.
 As Hunter S Thompson said, "the music business is a cruel and shallow money trench, a long plastic hallway where thieves and pimps run free, and good men die like dogs. There's also a negative side."

Or, as Les, former bassist with the luckless band Creme Brûlée from *The League of Gentleman*, put it with more slightly more brevity, "it's a shit business".

However, what people mean when they talk about 'the Music Industry' in these negative terms is often the large and successful parts of the recorded music business, and not all the other, sometimes benign and noble, stuff that happens elsewhere in what we should more accurately refer to as the Music Industries.

The recorded music business, as the name would suggest, is organised around the central idea of 'the record', and for that we must go back to Thomas Edison, who successfully managed to record the sound of his own voice saying the words 'Mary had a little lamb', in August 1878, and set in motion a chain of events that would eventually give the world the Spice Girls.

But there is also a positive side: the record, or 'the pop song', is the most democratic and versatile piece of art there has ever been.

It is the soundtrack to millions of lives, charts our loves and losses, and something that follows us and keeps us company from our wide-eyed, exuberant, youth to our befuddled and doddery old age. The experience you have when you hear a song is no more or less valuable than the experience it gives to millions of others. It's a *Living Thing*, as a famous Brummie once said, available to all, mostly cheap and, even when the songs themselves are sad, ultimately very, very, cheerful.

Edison kickstarted a process whereby musicians and singers could commit sound to permanent record that could be played back across time and space. Originally in the shape of wax cylinders, then in the form of actual records (made of various materials, but eventually vinyl), and then assorted other formats across the 20th century and into the new millennium. The process of committing glorious noise to 'record' has similarly evolved over time, from speaking into a horn, as Edison did, to multi-track tape recorders in fancy, expensive studios, to pinging music to collaborators across the world via the internet.

Much has changed since August 1878, then, but one thing has remained largely constant in the face of all these technological developments, economic progress and changing social conditions: pop songs are still (usually) under four minutes long. They have been for as long as anyone can remember, and probably always will be.

According to *The Billboard Experiment*, which analysed and then visualised sales charts and song information dating back to the birth of the pop charts, the average length of a hit record in the 1950s was two minutes and 36 seconds. Even though technology has developed at a huge rate since those days, the average length of pop songs today is still under four minutes and 30 seconds. Why is that?

It certainly has some roots in the restrictions of the technology of earlier times, both in terms of recording and playback mediums (you can only fit so many grooves on a record, after all), but the idea of pop being short, sharp and simple has, nevertheless, stuck.

Verse, Chorus, Verse, Chorus, Middle Eight, Chorus, Chorus — done. It's a straightjacket we no longer have to wear, but still do willingly. And, because of these restrictions, the restrictions of music itself, and of the copyright industry that underpins the business of recorded music, pop has had to be endlessly and fabulously inventive. That's why pop is great, bab.

There is, however, one particular point in the history of pop music when this brevity was temporarily bunged out the window, along with the idea of pop being a democratic, public art form belonging to us all... and that moment was called progressive rock, or prog.

Prog grew out of the notion of pop singers as artists that emerged in the 1960s around the likes of The Beatles and Bob Dylan. That, along with advances in studio technology and the realisation by the recorded music business that they could make more coin this way, led to the concept of 'the album' being the purest and highest form of the pop art.

From *Sgt. Pepper* it wasn't too great or long a leap to the idea of rock musicians as virtuosos, aloof and apart from the punters who worshipped them, of rock as high art that could only be understood in terms of it's ambition and scale. And also to Rick Wakeman's *King Arthur on Ice*.

Prog was endless noodling, complicated suites of music, and lyrics based on the worst kind of hobgoblin bothering nonsense imaginable, made by musicians from often highly privileged backgrounds. There were those that battled against this indulgence, including the caretaker of Birmingham Town Hall who locked up the organ and took the key home the night that Keith Emerson (of Emerson, Lake and Palmer) tried to play it — but it went on.

Prog eventually bored everyone so silly that we were forced to invent punk rock, which was also shit, but a least it was short shit, and that meant that everything was right with the world again.

Where on Middle Earth would a bunch of University-educated show-offs get the idea that people would be interested in overly-long fantasy bollocks? Step up to the mike, and strap on that double-necked guitar, J.R.R. Tolkien: the Brummie who hated Birmingham — who do you think the orcs are? — and almost helped to ruin pop music.

CH

No. 87: Feminist Journals

Hmmm — what to read? Celebrity cellulite hell; top-ten handbags-to-die-for; how to bake the perfect chocolate cheesecake; how to lose 15 stone in three days; how to perform the perfect blow-job; how to maintain the will to live...

Amidst today's flim-flam of celebrity, lifestyle, fashion and beauty publications consumed by much of British womanhood, there does exist progressive, political, publishing on women and their rights: and it is Birmingham, through one of its own daughters, that can proudly take the credit.

Long before there was *Spare Rib* (the late-lamented tribune of 1970s British second-wave feminism) there was *The English Woman's Journal* (1858-1864). This pioneering periodical was co-founded by Birmingham lass (albeit quite a posh one), Bessie Rayner Parkes, who was born in the city in 1829.

Her affluent, middle-class parents were Joseph Parkes, a solicitor of a radical political bent, and Elizabeth Rayner Priestley, granddaughter of scientist, philosopher and Unitarian minister, a chap you may have heard of: Joseph Priestley.

The family decamped to London in 1832, and then in 1847 to Hastings, where Bessie met Barbara Leigh Smith (later Bodichon) who became her lifelong friend and with whom she would later co-found The English Women's Journal.

Both women were thinkers and campaigners. In 1854, Bessie published her *Remarks on the Instruction of Girls*, on the need to broaden women's education to enable them to participate more fully in public life, and Barbara published *A Brief Summary of the Laws in England Concerning Women*, which resulted in 1857 in both women lobbying (unsuccessfully) to have parliament pass a Married Women's Property Act.

They founded the Journal the next year, publishing a mixture of political, social and literary content which reflected the social causes in which they were involved, and their determination to improve the lives and status of women in society. It was edited by Bessie, and supported by other proto-feminist activists of the time, who, from the Journal's offices ran *The Society for Promoting the Employment of Women*, with its women's employment agency, and related training schools, and campaigned on issues of women's work, suffrage, legal rights and education. Alright it's not diving under a racehorse, but this is pretty radical stuff.

In 1864, however, ongoing internal divisions between the Journal's chief supporters, ill-health on Bessie's part, and financial pressures all combined to bring about the end, and the Journal was dissolved. (In true publishing fashion, though, the title was amalgamated with another the next year — *Alexandra Magazine* — which morphed into yet another — *The English Woman's Review* — which continued in print until 1903, when it probably became *Razzle*.)

1865 saw the publication of Bessie's *Essays on Woman's Work*, some of which were taken from the journal. The

collection constituted a plea for more fulfilling lives
for middle-class women, and for better conditions
for working women. Rather sadly, perhaps, at least to
modern-day feminists, this was more or less the end of
Bessie's active involvement in the women's movement.
She converted to Roman Catholicism in 1864, married Frenchman Louis Belloc in 1867, living in France
for many years, and died in Sussex in 1925. Although
she continued to write, mainly poetry and reminis-
cences, it is for her championing of women's rights
through the written word that she will be remembered.
Oh, and being mother to poet, troublemaker, and we
learn, Brummie: Hilaire Belloc.

Today, no campaigning women's rights publication
aimed at a general readership in the UK currently
exists (an attempt to regenerate *Spare Rib* as an online,
crowdfunded journal lasted only from October 2013
to July 2014), and media reporting still tends to re-
flect the male experience as the norm, women's rights
issues are much more visible in the mainstream media.
Moreover, in academic circles, there are numerous
journals that adopt a feminist standpoint on a variety
of subjects, contributing to scholarship and learning,
and informing women's rights activism across the
globe.

Bessie, a product of Birmingham's 19th century liberal
middle-classes, created, through her *Women's English Journal*, the progenitor of contemporary feminist
publishing. And perhaps we can even see a nod to the
power of the feminist word in the let's face it, usually
mendacious, claims made to the 'empowering' nature
of the new lipstick/dress/botox treatment/lap-danc-

ing lesson that most of today's women's periodicals are trying to flog to us. She too had a lighter side, publishing in 1898 as Bessie R. Belloc, the no-doubt hilarious but sadly out of print *Historic Nuns*.

LC

No. 88: The White Line Down the Middle of the Road

To be a Cockney, you need to be born within earshot of the sound of the Bow bells. To be a Brummie, so Lawrence Inman's joke goes, you need to be born within earshot of someone moaning.

The truth, however, is somewhat cooler: Anyone can become a Brummie, and that's the beauty of it.

When outsiders do move to Birmingham — reluctantly or otherwise (although it's usually reluctantly) — they are indeed welcomed with open arms. All they have to do is ride a full circuit on the 11 bus and they can collect their lifetime Brummie pass. It's as simple as that. In truth, no-one actually checks if you've done the 11 thing, and most Brummies haven't done it themselves.

Once settled into their adopted city, these nu-Brummies begin to notice something strange: They find, perhaps in spite of themselves, that they begin to like the place.

When pressed on this, they will say things like, "Well, it's not as bad as I expected," which, whether these interlopers know it or not, is a very Brummie way of positively appraising a situation. Or, "the people are really nice… and they talk to you on the bus/in the street/at the shops", or, "It's a lot greener than I thought it would be". Slowly, but surely, we reel them in, just as we have done since the city was founded.

The newcomers also point out unlikely things. They point out things that the indigenous Brummie would miss, or not consider important, or not even dare to dream true. For example, one adopted Brummie I know, who spent a decade here, thinks the accent is a genuinely beautiful, lilting tone, and has described it as 'the English Italian'. Mind you, he was from <u>New Zealand</u> (a Brummie invention, incidentally) so perhaps he was just pleased to find a tribe of people who are more malicious to vowels than his own.

The other thing a lot of these adopted Brummies almost always point out is how crackers it is on the roads. Brummies, it seems, have what has been described by another outsider-cum-Brummie I know as a 'free jazz' approach to motoring. Birmingham is a town where 'No U-Turn' signs, for example, are an affront to the driver's inner Ornette Coleman and are often viewed and read as a direct challenge, rather than an instruction. As with the lilting accent compliment above, we're perhaps too close to notice this because we've lived with it all our lives, but it's probably true.

Whatever it is they teach you, for instance, about how to behave when negotiating roundabouts when you learn to drive is something we Brummies swiftly and proudly forget. This is highlighted by the fact that we, uniquely, refer to them by the more conceptual and poetic name of 'islands'. In fact, as any Brummie knows, the only real and true function of an 'island' is to provide, along with pubs, collectively understood points along an imaginary breadcrumb trail that enable us to give another Brummie directions from A to B in the city.

The irony in all of this motorised lawlessness is that road signs, whether they be warnings or general travel instructions in the form of images, collectively understood these days as 'street furniture', would not exist without the city of Birmingham.

It was here, in 1921, that following a series of traffic accidents at the junction of Maney Corner in Sutton that white lines were painted down the middle of the road, instructing drivers to keep to their lane and to WATCH IT. The experiment duly reduced low-speed pile ups between men in driving gloves and goggles and the practice quickly spread throughout the world. The rest is history and inevitable progress, and one that has recently returned to bite visitors to Birmingham in the wallet with the introduction of 200 metre long bus lanes that appear and disappear at the will of Birmingham City Council, who use them to fine unsuspecting drivers.

Beyond it's original motoring safety function, the white, centralised line — the middle of the road, in other words — has taken on a number of other, separate meanings throughout modern culture. A politician who deliberately occupies a position that makes them seen less of an arsehole than the others occupies 'the middle ground', for instance, just as a piece of popular culture, a film, or a pop song perhaps, that is inoffensive but entertaining is often said to be 'middle of the road'. No-one likes the middle of the road particularly, but there are sometimes worse places to be, and sometimes it's the best and most expedient place you can be. Which brings us back around to those newly arrived, newly minted Brummies.

So, next time you go out to or watch, listen, eat or vote for something, and upon reflection you find that it was dull, uninspiring, but, ultimately, not as bad as you were expecting, and if you then manage to make it home in one piece, just remember that you have Birmingham to thank for that entirely forgettable evening.

CH

No. 89: Looking Dapper

Hair is a problem. It sprouts from places you don't want it to, shies away from the top of your head (for us older men), and generally needs to be kept in its place. Regular barbering, or hairdressing for the ladies, is vital — as is plucking, shaving, combing over and other general topiary. Worse, even if it's perfectly in place when you leave the house one instance of hat usage, or any physical activity, can create a disaster of Johnsonian proportions.

Before 1928 there was no way of keeping hair under control: from Jesus, through Da Vinci to Wilfred Owen in the trenches of the Somme, all of society just looked a bit scruffy and unkempt. No wonder there was so much conflict.

But in that wonderful year Birmingham came to the rescue, as it always does. County Chemicals at their Chemico Works in Bradford Street formulated a pomade — an emulsion of water and mineral oil stabilised with beeswax — that, when spread across unruly follicles, truly made men look smart once and for all. They invented Brylcreem and the rest is neat, shiny, controlled history.

No idea how women manage mind you.

JB

No. 90: Speaking **YOUR** Brains

Jasper Carrott used to, and maybe still does, do a bit about a guy inadvertently swearing on local radio. The offender is new recruit sent out to report on a football match, and he almost manages to grab what will be a great bit of radio. In the days before outside broadcasting was easy he'd got one of the managers to agree to come to the phone to do an interview. This was all set up, and the studio was ready to come back to him after the news for his big moment.

Except the manager — probably Ron Saunders — got bored and left. "Tone, Tone, he's fucked off, Tone," broadcasts our hero.

The 'Tone' in question was Birmingham's own Tony Butler who bestrode local sports radio in the '70s and '80s and with one simple innovation changed the whole media landscape forever.

You would think that Tony would now be Director General of the BBC, or at least famous enough to be on gardening leave after some historic accusations. He's not, he stayed doing pretty much the same job until his retirement in 2013. At one point in the '90s Tony was promoted to the breakfast show on golden oldies station *XtraFM*, on this he unveiled his competition 'Butler's Bucket' in which listeners would have to guess what item was in his bucket. If this radio gold was cut short by someone guessing, then people would be asked to guess where in the West Midlands the bucket was.

And in that simplicity and interaction was Tony's genius: he let people phone up and say what they thought. He just put the public on the air: he invented the football phone-in.

From the humble beginnings of asking people to call BRMB and say that Ron Saunders was crap, the format exploded to fill every radio station, all of the time. Now there isn't a media outlet that doesn't ask YOU what YOU think so that you will happily fill THEIR air, inches or pixels with YOUR views about everything.

Tony Butler, in inventing the football phone-in, invented the future we live in. And he invented it for the people of Birmingham. And then, after doing it for decades, he fucked off. Tone.

JB

No. 91: 50 Shades of Grey

Every woman of a certain age wants to read about a 'red room of pain' it seems. Every supermarket bookshelf is filled with copies of the originally self-published and — apparently, I of course haven't read it — turgidly-written mommy-porn.

Just who'd have thought that some women would like reading about s-e-x? I don't know, what's the world coming to? I mean, isn't a quick look at Matt Berry showering in a sports vest on late night Channel 4 enough to keep them buzzing along? With or without batteries.

But it's really just a romance novel, not particularly sexily sexed up. And the progenitor of romance novels that really hit the spot? Dame Mary Barbara Hamilton Cartland, of course. Of Edgbaston, Birmingham, of course.

JB

No. 92: Little Tescos in Petrol Stations

"Does it have a mini-mart? A small supermarket, fits inside a garage, sells antifreeze and pasties, that type of thing?". The words of Alan Partridge back in 1997. One of the most loved traits of Partridge is his ability to highlight the absurdity of the banal. Partridge is in thrall to modernism but the modernism of the mundane is all that he can access, hence his affection for the supermarket-cum-garage.

I'm Alan Partridge arrived during a tipping point for the forecourt shop. In the 1990s a petrol station with a supermarket was a sophisticated new metropolitan invention and as such it was a staple of stand-up comedy routines — the gold standard being Eddie Izzard's surreal queue of murderers waiting at the late-night petrol station's hatch to buy a Twix. Petrol dispensing was, though, still an artisanal affair in many places in 1997.

For example, the petrol stations of my youth, far away from Birmingham:

There were two pumps. You drove in, your tyres crossed the pneumatic tube which made the bell ring and a young guy came out. "Fill her up please, with four star," you'd say. Some light chat, perhaps about the news, weather or football, then when you were done you'd pop into the little office. You'd hand over a few notes or perhaps you'd 'book it' (my local garage was the sort of place that did things on account).

There might be a few packets of sweets at the counter, and sundry motoring consumables like oil, tax disc holders and road atlases.

Those were the petrol stations of my youth. Those places were dying off in the 1990s though and the newer garages had more pumps, car parking, a cash point and where the small office used to be, there was a shop.

On my very first night in Birmingham, in 1997 as it goes, I arrived at the university's halls of residence in Perry Barr at about ten at night. I asked the girl who gave me my keys if there was a late night shop still open so I could get a cold drink and a snack. I was of course directed to a petrol station down the road. In Birmingham the petrol station had become the default mode of convenience shopping, somewhere you could walk to. This was Partridge's England, this was his modernity, this was his progress.

Nowadays when I go to the petrol station it's almost assumed I haven't come for fuel. "Any fuel with that today?" they ask as they bag my Hovis, my ready meal and its accompanying meal deal wine. And I've buzzed through that shop — for it's now a full blown shop they have at the garage, a Tesco store carrying everything I need — collecting those things in no time at all; in as much time as it used to take to pick up a pack of wine gums and book a tenner's worth of petrol to my parent's account I can fuel up and grab a basket full of groceries. That's why I'm pretty upset when this bloke storms in and says "Is that your fucking Mégane? Will you shift it I want some fucking petrol." "Mate," I say, "this is a supermarket, back off this is how it works now." He looks confused and a little ashamed as the other shoppers turn and glare at him, their baskets full of crumpets, pre-packaged sushi, Foster's lager and Kettle Chips. He throws his hands up in the air and storms back out again.

And that's a true story that took place at the Tesco in the Esso next to the Yenton in Erdington. Thinking back on it now I worry about that guy. Not for his impotent rage but because he's set against the march of progress. He's the same guy whose pub has been turned into a buffet Chinese restaurant. He's the guy whose nightclub is going to be turned into another coffee shop. He's the guy who'd like a toasted teacake but there's only fucking lovely cup cakes.

The forecourt office became a shop and then those shops became supermarkets. Systematically the big supermarkets dismantled an industry: the independent petrol station. I'm almost surprised we don't have a slow fuel movement, lobbying to bring it all back. But we don't. And although we have all read endless pieces in the newspapers about the supermarkets muscling in on books and DVDs or clothes and homeware, we never saw the broadsheet columnists standing up for the independently owned Texaco franchise. That's because there's a little bit of Partridge in all of us, I think, a little bit of us that's excited by the small supermarket that fits in a garage. And we get excited about all of this thanks, of course, to Birmingham.

Because you see Partridge's mini-mart owed its existence to the microwave oven which was the centrepiece of the shop. Here one could heat all manner of convenience goods sold within the store (as Alan often did). The microwave oven is an application of the cavity magnetron, invented in Birmingham in 1940 by John Randall and Henry Boot. Without the microwave oven the forecourt shop would have been grim indeed, but with it in place it gained a seductive modern air. Furthermore we can see that the push on to the development of larger shops, those little Tescos they have now, is also linked to this fine Brummie invention. For what is the little Tescos for if it is not for the sale of microwave ready meals, with a pudding, side and a bottle of wine for only £10? What you think this is a petrol station? Get a grip mate, and pop down the Chinese buffet for a pint.

JH

No. 93: Health and Safety

Used as a catch-all excuse for not letting people get on with things — in the same way as 'data protection' means people won't tell you things and political correctness means you simply aren't allowed to be a racist, cisexist, ableist, Islamophobe — like you could in the good old days, health and safety culture is one of the biggest influences on our lives. It's terrible that we're not at liberty to hurt ourselves and others and are given advice on how not to. Damn that health and safety, it's political correctness gone mad.

And you know who's to blame? Birmingham, that's who, er, where.

John Richard Dedicoat, an apprentice to the famous James Watt, became a bicycle manufacturer and, as well as inventing a spring-loaded step for mounting bikes — that charmingly catapulted riders over the handlebars if they misjudged it, he became the father of the nanny state with the invention of the bicycle bell. In one step he transferred the responsibility of pedestrian safety to the put-upon cyclist rather than the garrulous, attention-deprived, inconsiderate stroller. Damn Dedicoat and his pandering — safety should be the responsibility of the individual. Safety-fascists RO-SPA continue his legacy to this day, from Edgbaston.

Although some people think it would be frankly a lot safer if all the cyclists stayed at home.

HW

No. 94: Whistleblowing

If there's one thing you learn at school — and if the current government's Education department gets its way, you may only learn one thing — it's this: no one likes a tell tale tit. Watching *The Sweeney* you may have picked up this: nobody likes a grass. In fact, the only positive cultural representation of an informer that's easy to find is Starsky and Hutch's Huggy Bear, and you can bet that he had to run the gauntlet of hate from the other boss pimps in the area.

So, given that we don't like 'people what tell', how do we make sure that those in the know can reveal terrible problems in institutions without undue opprobrium? Back in the early '70s US civic activist Ralph Nader coined the phrase 'whistleblower' to avoid the negative connotations found in other words such as 'snitches'. He took his cue from the practice of giving a healthy toot on a whistle when there was a problem — be that a referee spotting a running back smacking a quarterback blind-side, offside (in the bastardisation of rugby that the yanks play), or the lookout on the Titanic seeing (all too late) a metric shittonne of ice.

Those metallic tooting machines — they came from Birmingham. The whistles on the Titanic were the famous Acme Thunderer, designed by Joseph Hudson's company. Hudson was a farm worker from Derbyshire who moved to the city like so many during the Industrial Revolution, and trained as a toolmaker.

He converted the wash house at the side of his end of terraced back-to-back home in St Marks Street into a workshop where he made many things to help increase his family's income. The company are still making a racket worldwide to this day — from Hockley.

JB

No. 95: Easy Listening

The commonly held view of 1960s popular music is that it was the decade during which the rulebook was torn up. Out of the dull austerity of the black-and-white '50s the youth of the following decade exploded as one in a Technicolor riot of mind-bending drugs, free love and revolutionary fervour. If you can remember it, you weren't there.

It was <u>The Beatles</u> who led the charge and provided the soundtrack, and nothing was ever the same again. As if to illustrate this point, Birmingham would give the world <u>heavy metal</u> by the end of the decade. But that's another story.

What this version of 1960s pop history doesn't tell us is that the rampaging youth were only part of the tale. There were also a lot of other people around in that decade, and many of them didn't much care for The Beatles and all they brought with them. Mostly these naysayers were drawn from the older generation (and in the 1960s, this meant anyone over the age of 21), and it rarely troubles the history books that they too, just like their younger counterparts, bought and listened to a lot of records.

What did these people want from pop music? It certainly wasn't sex, drugs and rock 'n' roll played by long-haired oiks, that's for sure. Indian spirituality? Womens' lib? Not their cup of cocoa. No, what they wanted was simply something pleasant they could tap their feet to: in a word, they wanted something nice.

That something nice came in the form of string-laden arrangements of pop hits, songs from the musicals, and movie soundtracks. No rough edges, and no feedback. It came to be known as Easy Listening, and the undisputed King of the genre was Annunzio Mantovani, or, as he was more commonly and simply known: Mantovani.

Mantovani had shifted a lot of records before the 60s even began. At one point in 1959 he had no fewer than six albums in the US Top 30 at the same time. This success continued throughout the next decade, when he became the first artist to sell a million stereo LPs, and with scarcely a burned bra in sight. In 1970, ten years before his death and a full four years before Kraftwerk hit upon a similar idea, he released *Music For The Motorway*, a suite of lushness inspired by the mundane joy of motorway travel. Travel sweets and driving gloves. Nice.

In terms of record sales, Mantovani was a behemoth. Remarkably, none of his light-orchestral unit-shifting niceness would have been possible without the city of Birmingham. In 1923, at the tender age of 18, Annunzio had cut his conducting teeth leading orchestras in the posh hotels of the city. The musicians he controlled were of a much older vintage and often included his father, Bismarck Mantovani (crazy name, crazy guy). Eventually, as with many Brum inventions before and since, the gifts outgrew the city of their birth and Mantovani was lured first to London, and then on to fame and fortune in the wider world.

We built this city on a toe-tapping tune, noice.   - *CH*

No. 96: The Last Night of The Proms

As the orchestra parps, the squiffy toffs bray, and the BBC commentators struggle with pitching their insight towards an audience that pretty much only wants to watch the *1812 Overture*, please remember to direct some of your swelling pooterish patriotism towards Birmingham. For without the global city there would be no local musical pride.

The Proms were launched in 1895 by some people in London, but they were not the first regular musical festival season, not by a long way. That may well have been the Birmingham Triennial Musical Festival which pre-dated the Proms by over one hundred years.

That first music festival in Birmingham, held over three days in September 1768, was to help raise funds to complete the new General Hospital on Summer Lane. It took another event ten years later in 1778 to achieve the funds to open the hospital in September 1779. A further five years on, in 1784, the performances became the Birmingham Triennial Musical Festival, and after naming it that they decided to run it every three years.

It was so bloody popular they built the Town Hall (in 1834) to house it, and it took the War to End All Wars to end it. But that spirit lives on, every September: with added plastic Union Jack bowler hats.

And the Last Night of those proms wouldn't be the same without the *Pomp and Circumstance* of one Edward Elgar who was Professor of Music at the University of — wait for it… — Birmingham. He wouldn't be where he is today without the city or its musical ambitions, four of his major choral works were commissioned by the Birmingham Triennial Music Festival.

Birmingham, land of hope and glory.

JB

No. 97: The Inevitable Downfall of the BBC

It's amazing that, with the modern attention span the way it is, the BBC has managed to keep any programme going for over 60 years. That's a testament to a wonderful variety of writers, producers, and editors, it's a tribute to the management that held faith and more than anything it's a case study in how taking a punt on an innovative idea can produce something astounding.

The Archers, recorded in the Borsestshire village of Ambridge — but produced and broadcast from the nearby big city of Birmingham — is not only wonderful entertainment, but was the world's first 'scripted reality' show. The genre, with *The Only Way Is Essex*, *Geordie Shore* and *Midlands Today* all riding high in the ratings, feels like the very definition of NOW: but did you know it started in May of 1950 for those of us in the Midlands, and on 1 January 1951 for the rest of the country? We've all been listening for 64 years and counting, or maybe it just feels like that.

But innovative and important though it is, *The Archers'* tales of everyday country folk are a pernicious cancer at the heart of our Public Service Broadcasting.

The series was originally produced with 'input' from the Ministry of Agriculture, Fisheries and Food, leading to pressure on the producers to feed lines to the villagers. Some conspiracy theorists, the same ones that claim not to be able to find Ambridge on a map, say that whole episodes and storylines have been carefully scripted — although we see no evidence of this.

The government's angle was to disseminate 'information to farmers and smallholders to help increase productivity in the post-World War II years of rationing and food shortages', which may have been true at the time. The state interference in the media in this case is very much the thin end of the wedge: which is a term used to describe a practice that is likely to get worse and not a polite Radio 4 way of referring to Walter Gabriel's 'old pal', me old beauty.

The ability to nudge the listener by nudging the people of Ambridge sent the corporation a little power crazy. We all remember the scandals over phone-in competitions and the like. After investigations by the tabloids it turned out that everyone from Lord Reith to Bob Monkhouse had at some point had their fingers in the till (or in something else entirely): and it's hard to think that someone at the BBC isn't getting a backhander from sales of Tom Archer's organic wieners.

Having got away with it here, it was a short step to installing a former Young Conservative Chairman as chief political editor and completely neutering the entire organisation's news output under the pretext of the Hutton Inquiry.

We can balance these black sheep in the BBC flock with the wonderful example of diversity that the village shows the rest of Britain: the array of accents on the programme is tremendous — as is the effort that some of the stars show in vocalising their actions for the radio, even when clearly suffering from breathing difficulties. It's not uncommon to hear a Midlander, a Geordie, a Londoner and someone who has watched too much of Russ Abbott's C.U. Jimmy character all in one pub conversation. This is tremendous, not only for multiculturalism but also as it's much easier to tell the people apart than it is on *Made in Chelsea*.

The Archers, then, it opened the door for the sort of meddling that will eventually kill the BBC, but it is a wonderful mirror to society. And we have Birmingham to thank.

JB

No. 98: Pointless Kitchen Appliances

Everyone has a guilty secret tucked away in the hardest to reach cupboard of their kitchen. Is yours a donut maker, a Breville or a pasta machine? The answer will depend very much on your age, your class, and when you reached key milestones in your life course but most certainly you have them. Did you marry in the 1970s? You have a fondue kit. Were you a student in the noughties? You have a chocolate fountain. Hit 30 in the late 1990s? That sudden paunch made you invest in a smoothie maker (but didn't make you stop to think about quite how much sugar there is in a smoothie).

Let's go through the Kay's catalogue of the mind and think about some of the other ridiculous single-use gadgets that have come into our homes, been unboxed, used once and then packed away to the high shelf: bread machine, cup cake maker, slow cooker, rice cooker, coffee percolator, milk frother, ice cream maker, food processor, coffee grinder, spice mill… an endless list of useless crap. Most of these things duplicate things that our main appliances already do: the cooker, the kettle, a fucking *knife*. We buy, we use, we realise our mistake and we swear we'll never again be seduced by the marketing patter of 'convenience', the marketing patter that started here in Birmingham.

You see people have been able to make toast for centuries. It's a simple process: apply a radiant heat to a slice of bread. You can do it over a fire and you can do it under a grill. None of that stopped the guys at Birmingham based Bullpitt & Sons Ltd from inventing the toaster which they sold under the Swan brand (they also really pushed things forward with the Teasmade).

That's right, it took Brummie engineering and chutzpah to design and then sell you a machine to do the things you could already do, and in doing so they invented a new category of device: the fundamentally useless kitchen gadget.

This gift reaches further than just to the cupboard out in the utility room where your George Formby Grill lives next to your deep fat fryer. If it wasn't for the fundamentally useless kitchen gadget, would we have eBay? It's doubtful, isn't it? And how about the car boot sale? The useless kitchen gadget is the mainstay of these secondary market places. When Swan invented the toaster they can't have possibly dreamed how much they would change the world because after all: what is the actual point of a toaster when you have a cooker with a grill?

JH

No. 99: The Cardboard Box

When Charles Henry Foyle invented the cardboard box, in Birmingham, in the late 19th century, he by turn invented supermarkets: for would they be able to pile 'em high and sell 'em cheap if they didn't pile neatly in cartons and boxes?

They, including Jack Cohen who came up with that motto and founded Tesco, would not have been able to. That the real idea turned out to be to pile 'em high, sell 'em cheap, force other smaller retailers of 'em out of business, before using your virtual monopoly of 'em to control both supply of 'em and the eventual higher price of 'em isn't Charles Henry Foyle's fault. He just originated the process that made manufacture of brightly coloured containers to put 'em in cost effective. They call it the 'folding carton'.

Charles was lucky to be in Birmingham. Birmingham as we've discovered is a place where lots of people invent lots of things. And those things that aren't cultural concepts, or gases, or types of buildings, or sports, often need boxes to put them in. In Birmingham he had <u>bicycle bells</u> and <u>kettles</u>, and <u>shit shoes</u> to make boxes for. if he'd lived in <u>Manchester</u> or London what would there have been to box up? Cotton? Rain? Alan Sugar's wolf-like hands pointing across a glass table?

The invention of the box, and the founding of the excellently named Boxfoldia Ltd made a fortune as well as the future. If you've been to the MAC or the Birmingham Museum and Art Gallery then you've shared in those profits too: Charles Foyle used some of his wealth to start a trust for the good of the city, one that's still going nearly 70 years after his death.

A renaissance man as well as a philanthropist, Charles privately published *Alice Through The Paper-Mill*, an *Alice In Wonderland* inspired satire on war-time paper control regulations — a delicious subject for humour. No doubt he had to lean heavily on brothers William and Gilbert who had founded Foyle's bookshop in London to stock it.

The book contains a chapter where Alice exclaims to one of the odd inhabitants of the world, "I thought you'd gone to Reading?", the very idea of which is so surreal it rather makes the whole book seem unlikely. Even when Boxfoldia Limited was resurrected a couple of years ago — it had lasted until 2005 when it was liquidated — it only went as far as Redditch.

JB

No. 100: The United States of America

Oh, America: hamburgers, hot rods, hanging out at the mall, rock 'n' roll, *Fox News*, an out-of-control culture of gun violence. You've come a long way since you were a just another undiscovered continent of perfectly happy indigenous tribes.

Your star may now be on the wane, but you won't find many people who will disagree with the notion that the 1900s were very much the American century. It was when you grew so strong, so big, and so quickly, that your power was undeniable. Culturally, economically, militarily — there was no-one to touch you. You even reached for the stars and lassoed the moon. Well done, America.

There are some who may argue that your rampant success was built on the foundations of your early life as a colony of Britain. After all, it was the British who gave you your language, your ingenuity, and your pioneer spirit. But to claim this stellar rise to success was the result of British intervention would be tenuous, to say the least. No, in truth, it wasn't until you struck out on your own and decided to make a fist of it that you truly realised your potential.

So, how did you do it?

How did you take those first steps? And, once on that road to freedom, what informed the creation of your culture? What enabled you to become the dominant nation of the world? Well, America, your history books may not tell you this but it was, as it happens, the city of Birmingham.

Two of your founding fathers, Benjamin Franklin and Thomas Jefferson, got their revolutionary ideas and zeal from their involvement with Birmingham's Lunar Society, the ad hoc collection of political, economic, mechanical and cultural minds that formed in the city in 1765 and which managed, through a process of free-thinking, a spirit of open-mindedness, and a middle finger firmly raised in the direction of the status quo, to pretty much invent the modern world that you eventually dominated.

From their visits to Birmingham in the 1700s, Jefferson and Franklin took this free-wheeling spirit and a belief in the right to free assembly back home with them. To defend this right, they wrote into your constitution the right to bear arms. There would be no arms to bear if not for us, for it was here, in Birmingham, that the guns, and the <u>hand grenades</u>, and the nuclear missiles that are variously used (or not used) in the defence of freedom, initially came into being.

Your first great export to the world was <u>cinema</u> (impossible without Birmingham), through which you invented the teenage rebel who shocked square society. The rebels rode motorbikes (a Brummie innovation) in the '50s, and rode them still as they evolved into the counter-cultural hippies of the late '60s (channelling that Lunar Society vibe once more). Far out, bab.

Those hippies then cut their hair and started working in the <u>banks</u> (another Brummie invention) that became economic powerhouses, whilst your manufacturing processes took the (Brummie) innovations of the Industrial Revolution to hitherto unseen levels of growth and efficiency. In turn this created the disposable income that your brands, such as the carbonated (yes, that's right) <u>Coca Cola</u>, successfully fought over on their way to conquering the world.

By the early 1980s, it was all over — there was truly no-one to touch you. And it is surely no coincidence, either, that around this time you took (Birmingham's) Duran Duran to your hearts in a way that we never could. Thus the baton was passed and the process of your Brum-inspired rise to global prominence was complete.

If you've ever wondered why you instinctively treat Ozzy Osbourne like royalty, now you know: it's in the genes.

So, America, on 4 July next year, raise a glass to your hometown, and don't forget the high foive.

CH

No. 101: A Nice Cup of Tea and a Sit Down

There is a very simple principle to the making of tea and it's this: to get the proper flavour of tea, the water has to be boiling (not boiled) when it hits the tea leaves. If it's merely hot then the tea will be insipid.

A watched pot never boils but an electrical kettle does, and so every properly nice brew has poured from the over-flowing cup of wonders that is Birmingham. That's right, the science behind the modern electric kettle — and a decent cuppa — comes from Brum. Arthur Large created an immersed heating element and the boffins at Bullpit & Sons added a cut-off valve. Thus was born the nice cup of tea and a sit down and, with it, the space to think and ponder, to reframe the problem that you can't solve while you refresh your mind and body.

How many more great ideas and inventions stand on the shoulders of this giant? How many innovations would not have come to fruition but for a soothing cup of PG Tips?

Too many to count — and this time we're only going up to 101.

JH

You Have Been Watching

Jon Bounds (JB), Jon Hickman (JH), Craig Hamilton (CH), Danny Smith (DS), Julia Gilbert (JG), Simon Fox (SF), Libby Hayward Bounds (LHB), Stuart Harrison (SH), Jez Collins (JC), Liz Cooke (LC), Steve Nicholls (SN), Jon Neale (JN), Nick Stevens (NS) and Howard Wilkinson (HW).

Cover design by Mark Murphy.

Edited by Jon Bounds and Jon Hickman, from an original idea by Craig Hamilton.

Additional editorial support from Libby Hayward Bounds, Julia Gilbert, and Nick Moreton.

Thanks To

We couldn't have done it without Wikipedia [no citation needed] nor the support of Kickstarter backers, including these guys:

- Adam Green
- Adam Stewart
- Alan McCann
- Andy Howlett
- Ben Waddington
- Blake Woodham
- Bren
- Brian Simpson

- Camilla Neppl Huber
- Caroline
- Cath Palgrave
- Christian Rusty Holloway
- Christopher Tsouvallaris
- Christopher Williams
- Claire Margaret Genevieve Spencer
- Damion Rice
- Dan Slee comms2point0
- Darren Langley
- Daryl Tomkins
- Dave Brown
- David Fisher
- David Goodman
- David Sagstad
- Derick
- Dubber
- Ed Cook
- Ed Lacey
- Eddie Bilborough
- Gary Ashwin
- Hannah Bounds
- Harry Vale
- Jake Grimley
- James Cook
- James McMullan
- Jamie Bullock
- Jamie McLeod
- Janine Wiedemann
- Jess Phillips
- Jez Higgins
- John Paddington
- Julia Gilbert
- Lee Mostari

- Margaret Roper
- Marie Pawlowski
- Mark Burge
- Mark Rogers
- Matthew Gidley
- Michael Loftus
- Michael Ware
- Michelle M Rafferty
- Mr KD Butt Esq
- Neil "I'm only a flipping philanthropist now!" Hine
- Nick
- Owen Johnson
- Paul Scott
- Peel and Stone
- Pete and Fiona
- Pete Stevens
- Peter Allen
- Phil Berry
- Rachel
- Rachel Cockett
- Raffaela Goodby
- Rebecca Roden
- Richard Phipps
- Robert Pugsley
- Robert Rowe
- Robin from Brum
- Sam Todd
- Sasha Kelley
- Simon & Katie
- Simon Fox
- Siôn Perks
- Steve "steviesocial" Jones
- Steven D Quirke
- Stuart Hackney

- Stuart Harrison
- Thomas T. Parker
- Tim Ellis
- Tom Ebbutt
- Tony Barnett
- Tony Smith
- Wendy Lowes

Paradise Circus

www.paradisecircus.com

A Birmingham Miscellany, Paradise Circus is an ongoing love letter to a battered city. It writes, makes and records things about Birmingham.

16667662R00134

Printed in Great Britain
by Amazon